BELFAST CITY HALL

An Architectural History

Paul Larmour

ULSTER ARCHITECTURAL
HERITAGE SOCIETY

Published 2010 by the
Ulster Architectural Heritage Society
66 Donegall Pass, Belfast
with the support of Belfast City Council

British Library Cataloguing in Publication Data
A catalogue record for this book is available from the British Library

Designed by April Sky Design, Newtownards
Printed by W&G Baird Ltd, Antrim

ISBN: 978-0-900457-72-2 (softback)
978-0-900457-73-9 (hardback)

Large Format Landmark series No. 2
General Editor: Terence Reeves-Smyth

Front Cover:
View of Belfast City Hall from North-West [Chris Hill]

Back Cover:
The dome interior viewed from the entrance hall [Author, 2009]

Frontispiece:
Belfast City Hall, 1906 [Welch Collection, Ulster Museum]

Tailpiece:
The Belfast Arms in a window of the main staircase. The motto translates
as 'What return shall we make for so much?' [Author, 2009]

CONTENTS

FOREWORD

The City Hall marks the physical centre of Belfast, but it has also been at the core of life in Belfast since it opened over a hundred years ago. The building's importance to the city and the affection in which it is held came through very strongly during the centenary celebrations. This was reinforced by the way so many missed the Hall when it was closed for the recent major refurbishment and in the enthusiasm with which its re-opening was greeted. The recent work means that not only is the City Hall fit for work in the 21st century, it probably looks better than it has at any time since 1906.

Given the scale, splendour and importance of the City Hall, it seems strange that there has been no extended consideration of its architecture before Dr Larmour's splendid piece of research. Even for those of us who know this great building very well, there are revelations on almost every page. The author connects Belfast's gem to the wider story of western architecture, bringing out the ambition of both the architect and those who commissioned him. Belfast people are proud of their City Hall and they now have access to information which validates and explains many of the reasons why. The beauty of the building is undeniable, but anyone who reads this book will have a better understanding of the structures which lie underneath the surface and the inspired design which has brightened citizens' lives for so long.

Belfast City Council is delighted to have supported this book and grateful to Dr Larmour, the Ulster Architectural Heritage Society, and everyone who has put in so much hard work to bring the publication into being.

Cllr Naomi Long
Lord Mayor

November 2009

TO LYNNE

PREFACE

This book describes the history and architecture of the building which for over a century has not only served as the headquarters of Belfast City Council, but has also stood as an icon for the city and a symbol of its civic pride and progress.

Belfast City Hall is both a civic monument and an artistic legacy for the city, which has long deserved a more complete photographic and written record than hitherto. The centenary occasion of its initial building marked a milestone in its history, which seemed to offer the most timely opportunity to redress the balance, but for various reasons it had to wait. Now, following the recent refurbishment and tasteful repainting, coming after some decades of unsatisfactory colour schemes, and with the building looking as fresh inside as it must have done when first opened, the time to pay tribute seems opportune again.

The book is planned as both a history of the original project from inception to completion, and a guide to the building today. Its publication has been made possible by a generous grant from the City Council, for which the Ulster Architectural Heritage Society and I thank them and their Chief Executive, Mr. Peter McNaney.

For my part, I also wish to thank the following individuals for particular assistance: Ivan Kirkpatrick, Robert Watton, Robert Corbett, Robert Heslip and Diane Leeman, all of the City Council, for access to original drawings and archival photographs, and Robert Corbett also for pointers to some historical sources; Peter McKay of the City Council for granting freedom to visit all parts of the building; John Savage of Consarc, architects for the refurbishment of the building from 2007-2009, for his generosity of time in conducting me around the building during the course of that contract when it was otherwise closed to the public; Ian Montgomery and Gemma McCallion of the Public Record Office of Northern Ireland for providing access to the uncatalogued drawings deposited there by the City Council; David Griffin and Anne Henderson of the Irish Architectural Archive in Dublin, and Trevor Parkhill and Michelle Ashmore of the Ulster Museum, for assistance with some archival illustrations; Professor Fred Boal, Professor Alun Evans, Chris Hill, and Blackstaff Press for permission to reproduce various illustrations; Gareth Edwards of NIEA for scanning my slides; and Karen Latimer and Gordon Wheeler for helping to copy edit the text.

A particular expression of thanks is due to Terence Reeves-Smyth, publications editor of the UAHS, for assistance with the acquisition of other archival photographs, for useful suggestions regarding the text, for masterminding the format and layout of the book, for liaising with the designers, April Sky Design, and for his part in securing the all-important publications grant, for which I am also very grateful to Nick Hanna and Primrose Wilson, chairwoman of the UAHS.

Dr Paul Larmour

1st October 2009

INTRODUCTION

As Rome has St Peter's, and London has St Paul's, so Belfast has the City Hall, a magnificent architectural centrepiece in Classical style crowned by a massive and eye-catching dome whose dominant form provides the city with its enduring and defining image.

Belfast City Hall is a truly noble building. It was designed in 1896 by a then relatively unknown English architect, Alfred Brumwell Thomas, to whom it eventually brought fame and a knighthood when it opened in 1906.[1]

A municipal palace built on a really grand scale, its story is one of a long drawn out construction process during which the design underwent many changes, all for the better, while the cost escalated to unsuspected heights, something which raised objections at the time, but eventually was merely to add to both its allure and its esteem. It is also a story of a growing sense of civic pride which made the building's final grandiose form almost an inevitability, the crowning achievement of a very successful and indeed unprecedented period of progress for the city.[2]

When the first corporation for Belfast had been elected in 1842, the population was just over 75,000. At the time their council premises was a rented building in Poultry Square, later known as Victoria Square, containing only one large meeting room and six offices, together with a police office and cells. It proved to be inconvenient for what was becoming a growing town and within only a decade there was a plan to replace it.

In 1852 William Hastings, the town surveyor, proposed a design for a new town hall for Belfast in Corinthian style, for which, prophetically, the circular porches on the transepts of St Paul's Cathedral in London were to be one of the sources.[3] It was intended to be sited on the west bank of

the River Lagan, to the south of Queen's Bridge, but it came to nothing; likewise, a project by the Belfast architect Thomas Turner, first mooted in 1856, but resurrected in 1866. This latter scheme envisaged replacing the White Linen Hall in Donegall Square with 'a grand group of public buildings with the town-hall in the centre, the railings and trees cleared, and the space opened and beautified by statues of eminent men'.[4]

Turner's idea for a site was ahead of its time in light of future developments, but when a competition was held in 1869 for a new town hall to replace the old Victoria Square premises, it was decided to build it in Victoria Street. Designed by the local architect Anthony Jackson and finished in 1871, it provided not only a town hall with offices for several departments, but also three court-rooms, together with a police office and cells, and a fire-station.

Two-storeyed, built of red sandstone in a fairly plain Romanesque style, the new town hall was of such proportions, however, that even when first built it was criticised by some townspeople as not displaying sufficient dignity or ostentation. It had originally been designed with the roof rising from plain eaves, but 'the townspeople protested that it was not a public building not having a parapet; and so great was the agitation that the plans had to be submitted to the Treasury for consideration'[5] and the parapet was duly added.

On a more practical level the expansion of Belfast continued to be so rapid during the later nineteenth century, with ever rising population levels to match its industrial and commercial growth, that only a decade or so later this new building was found to be inadequate for its municipal function, being so cramped that it could not accommodate all the council's officials.

Top: *Former Town Hall, Victoria Street, 1869-71, by Anthony Jackson [MBR, Belfast]*

Bottom: *Former Town Hall, Victoria Street: interior of the Council Chamber around 1900 [Welch Collection, Ulster Museum]*

Top: *The White Linen Hall, Donegal Square, built in 1785: the main entrance front in the late 1880s [MBR, Hill Street]*

Bottom: *The White Linen Hall: the courtyard sometime after 1888 [Welch Collection, Ulster Museum]*

It still stands, but is now used as a court house.

The growing town of Belfast had become a city, by royal charter, in 1888. By this time it was the chief seat and trading centre of linen production in the world, and in the front rank for shipbuilding, marine engineering and machine making, and was a leader in rope making, distilling and tobacco manufacture. The ever-increasing requirements of the city, with a population of over 200,000 in the 1880s, now meant there was a growing necessity for a more spacious and modern building for municipal business than the old town hall; it also meant there was an increasing desire to symbolise the wealth and importance of the community in a much more palatial and prestigious civic building than hitherto.

The swell of opinion in favour of a new city hall led to the Corporation's Law and Improvement Committee entering into a provisional agreement in 1889 for the purchase of the premises of the old eighteenth-century White Linen Hall, in Donegall Square, as a site for the intended new building. The White Linen Hall was a two-storeyed quadrangular building of mainly utilitarian appearance, though it boasted a pedimented centrepiece with a surmounting clock tower. It had been built in 1785 as a distribution centre for the local linen industry.[6] With the advent of large warehouses for individual firms elsewhere in the surrounding streets from the mid-nineteenth century onwards, however, the White Linen Hall had ceased to be an important central market and had outlived its original purpose. The Countess of Shaftesbury, whose family still owned the site, had wanted the old buildings to be demolished and the entire grounds to become a public park,

but she had been persuaded that its central position offered a convenient site for a new city hall and so had agreed to the Corporation's proposal to build there. The surrounding area, which had once been largely residential, had become increasingly used for commercial and financial purposes, so the site seemed ideal for the Corporation's purposes.

In July 1890 the necessary Parliamentary sanction was obtained, by the passing of an act, to authorise the transfer of the land to the Corporation, at a cost of £30,000. In October 1893 the Corporation's Improvement Committee recommended that plans for a new city hall should be invited, especially as the city's tramway rent would be available the next year so that the cost of the building could be provided without increasing taxation. However, the Corporation decided to wait.[7] Then a year later, in October 1894, a resolution was passed announcing the Council's determination to build a new city hall. There was a delay in demolishing the old buildings, however, caused by the Council permitting the Working Men's Institute to hold an industrial exhibition there from April to September 1895. Eventually the site was cleared by February 1896 when the last of the tenants moved out.

The way was now open to pursue the Corporation's long-discussed aim to erect new headquarters. Here for the first time could be brought together all the Corporation departments which had hitherto been housed in different premises around the city. At the same time the new building could give proud visible expression to Belfast's status as the third highest revenue-paying city in the United Kingdom.

A GREAT ENTERPRISE

Previous Page: *The centrepiece of the City Hall with the statue of Queen Victoria standing in front of it [Author, 2006]*

THE COMPETITION

A formal decision to build a city hall was made by the City Council at a meeting in January 1895, when it was also agreed that a competition should be held for the design. By November that year it had been further decided that the cost of the loan to be obtained for the building would be met out of the profits of the city's gas undertaking. Soon after, in December 1895, a sub-committee[8] was formed and met with the city surveyor J.C. Bretland in order to determine the block plan and the detailed requirements for the accommodation, and, in an attempt to ensure that the competition would be conducted on the best lines possible, the draft conditions were to be forwarded to the Royal Institute of British Architects for further suggestions including the nomination of an assessor.

The position the building was to occupy on the site had given rise to considerable discussion both inside and outside the Council. A view held by many people was that it should face Donegall Square West with its back to Donegall Square East, so as to allow the main thoroughfare of Donegall Place to be continued on through to Linenhall Street. In the end the majority opinion was in favour of the position in which the building now stands: that is, set back to Donegall Square South, facing Donegall Square North and closing the vista from Donegall Place.

By June 1896 Alfred Waterhouse, President of the Royal Institute of British Architects, and himself architect of some of the finest municipal buildings in Great Britain,[9] had been nominated and duly appointed as assessor for the competition, to be assisted by J.C. Bretland. In

July 1896 designs for the proposed building were invited through the architectural press,[10] with a closing date of 25th October that year.

It was to be a two-stage competition: as the advertisement stated, 'from among the sketch designs so sent in, three will be selected for a further and final competition'. The sum of £300 was offered in premiums, to be divided equally between those competitors who would satisfy the requirements of the final competition. There was however the proviso that the architect of the adopted design would have his prize money merged with his fees, which would be five per cent on the amount of the tender accepted for the erection of the building. The cost of constructing the general fabric of the building was not to exceed £125,000, 'and including all special features, architectural embellishments, and permanent fittings', was not to exceed the sum of £150,000 overall.

Printed conditions, together with a block plan showing how much space could be devoted to the new building, and sketch plans showing the suggested accommodation, were available to all intending competitors.[11]

Bretland's sketch plans were little more than diagrammatic, and his arrangement of three entire storeys throughout led to a few spaces being labelled as 'spare', but the aim was clearly to establish particular key rooms in a proportionate way. The task for the competitors, of course, was to weld the volumes into a more cohesive and consummate whole, from what was officially only a schedule of accommodation. Yet, in the light of the eventual winning entry, there were clearly the germs of some useful concepts in the diagrams. Such features as projecting corner blocks, an almost continuous system of quadrangular corridors, a distinct separation of departmental offices, the treatment of the first floor as a *piano nobile* or principal floor containing large public rooms to the front, and the expansive treatment of a centrally placed main entrance area with a main staircase, side lobbies and a surrounding gallery, with a *porte cochère* to the front, all contained within Bretland's guidelines, were subsequently to be adopted in the winning entry.

No restrictions were imposed as regards the style of the building, but it was stressed that preference would be given to designs treated in 'a bold dignified manner' and that 'from the nature of the site, each façade must be treated as important'. It was also required that the building should be of fireproof construction.

The unrestricted and open nature of the site together with complete stylistic freedom appeared to offer a great opportunity to competitors, yet almost immediately there was disquiet at some of the published conditions. *The Builder*, the

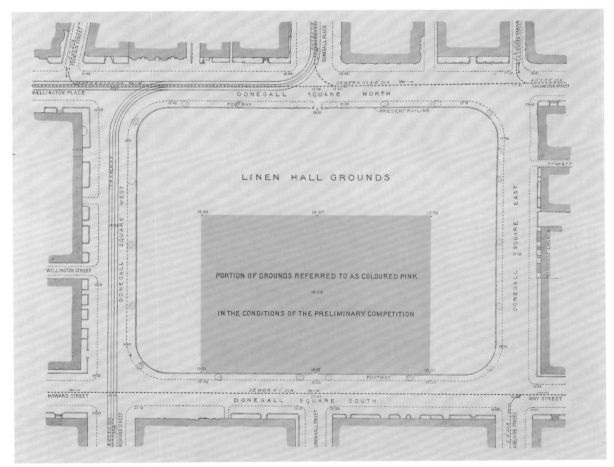

Left: *Block plan showing proposed site, by J.C. Bretland, 1896. [PRONI]*

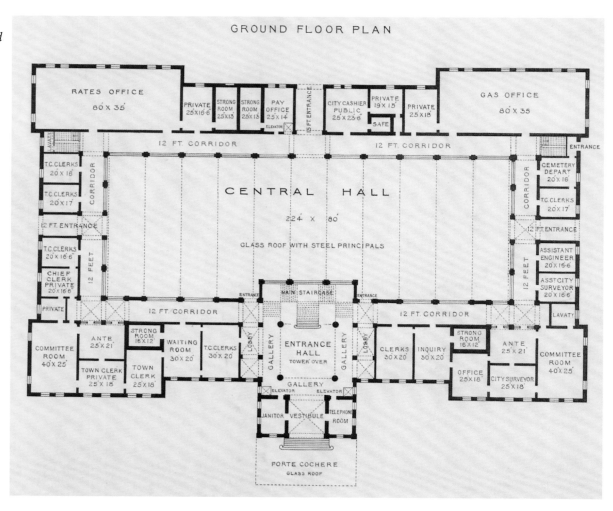

leading British architectural journal of the time, which was published in London, disapproved in particular of the decision to limit the selected architect's expenses for travel.

This objection was repeated in letters from some leading members of the profession in Britain, including the prominent Scotsman, John Brydon, who was indignant enough to declare that he was declining to enter the competition in protest.[12]

The competition committee of the Royal Institute of British Architects found itself under attack from various correspondents over the matter to such an extent that its chairman, Charles Barry, felt compelled to explain in the press that while they had been asked by Belfast Corporation to help draft conditions, some of

their advice had been ignored. Thomas Drew, a leading Irish architect, originally from Belfast but then based in Dublin, echoed in a letter to the *Irish Builder* in October 1896, the general sentiments of the main objectors in Britain, who included John Brydon, his fellow Scot, William Young, and the well-known English architect John Belcher. Wisely however, Drew also urged calm, suggesting that the apparently objectionable clause about travelling expenses could probably be sorted out later.[13]

In the event, there were fifty-one entries, drawn from England and Scotland as well as from Ireland. By early November 1896 Waterhouse was in Belfast to judge them, with the assistance of Bretland.[14] The initial task of the assessors was to choose three designs which could then

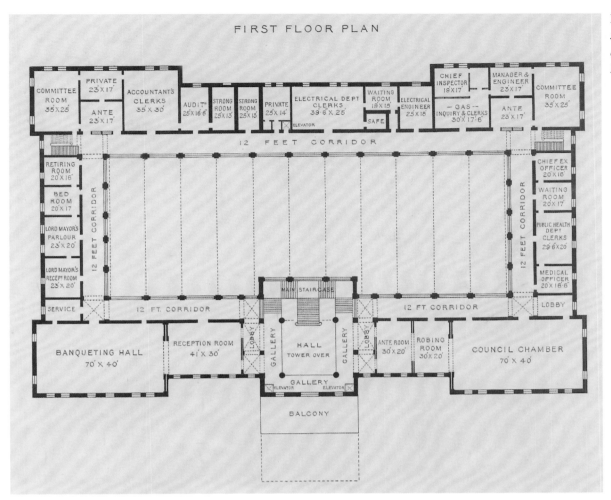

FIRST FLOOR PLAN

Left: *Sketch plan showing suggested first floor accommodation, by J.C. Bretland, 1896 [PRONI]*

be amended if necessary before a final decision would be taken. The three entries selected for the second or final stage of the competition were those of E. Thomas & Son of London, Stark & Rowntree of Glasgow, and James Miller of Glasgow.

Controversy arose, however, at a meeting of the City Council on 13th November when the three finalists' officially selected entries were to be examined by the members, but two more sets of drawings were added, bringing the number in the final stage up to five.[15] One of these extras, both of which were added without the authority of the assessors and beyond the terms of the competition, was from the Belfast firm of Graeme-Watt & Tulloch.[16] They had followed Bretland's suggested arrangements of accommodation very closely, including a large public hall in the centre

of an otherwise quadrangular layout. This clearly appealed to some members of the Council, who were led to intervene, encouraged no doubt by a certain element of partisanship.

In a further development, at a meeting of the Council on 30th November, these five entries were looked at by the members again, and in a vote taken to determine a final three, while the position of two of the original finalists, Stark & Rowntree, and James Miller, was confirmed, the remaining one of the originally approved three, E. Thomas & Son, had now been displaced by Graeme-Watt & Tulloch. It was this altered decision by the Council, rather than that of the official assessors, which was almost immediately broadcast in the press,[17] so, although Graeme-Watt & Tulloch, uneasy about the revelations, quickly made it known that they were withdrawing from the competition,[18] and were acknowledging the original decision of the assessors, it was too late to avoid the inevitable embarrassment of having their names linked with a blatant case of interference in the proceedings. Against a background of mounting criticism from various quarters, the Council then met on 7th December and confirmed Waterhouse's original selection of three finalists.[19]

Following this first stage of the competition, it was decided that the provision of a large hall in the building should be one of the conditions of the final stage. The City Council had not then become owners of the Ulster Hall, a large public meeting hall in Bedford Street, dating from 1859-62, or this addition to the accommodation might not have been deemed necessary at any stage of the competition.

That the three selected finalists had all initially omitted a central hall, while a number of other competitors had opted to include one, in itself led to a certain amount of controversy at the time, with various letters sent to the Press from disgruntled parties complaining that the indication of a central hall in Bretland's sketch plan surely implied a definite need for one.[20]

Eventually, in March 1897, after the selected schemes had been amended, the assessors considered them and adjudged E. Thomas and Son to be the winners.[21] They explained their findings in a confidential report to the members of the Council on 17th March:

'The three competitors have all sent in the prescribed drawings for the final competition together with those which set forth their design in the first instance. For the most part, in our opinion, the amended

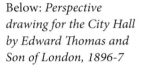

Below: *Perspective drawing for the City Hall by Edward Thomas and Son of London, 1896-7*

NEW TOWN HALL, BELFAST. W.L.

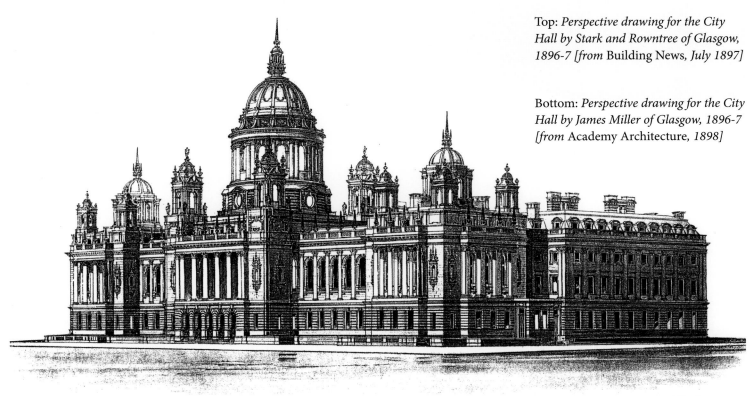

Top: *Perspective drawing for the City Hall by Stark and Rowntree of Glasgow, 1896-7 [from* Building News, *July 1897]*

Bottom: *Perspective drawing for the City Hall by James Miller of Glasgow, 1896-7 [from* Academy Architecture, *1898]*

23

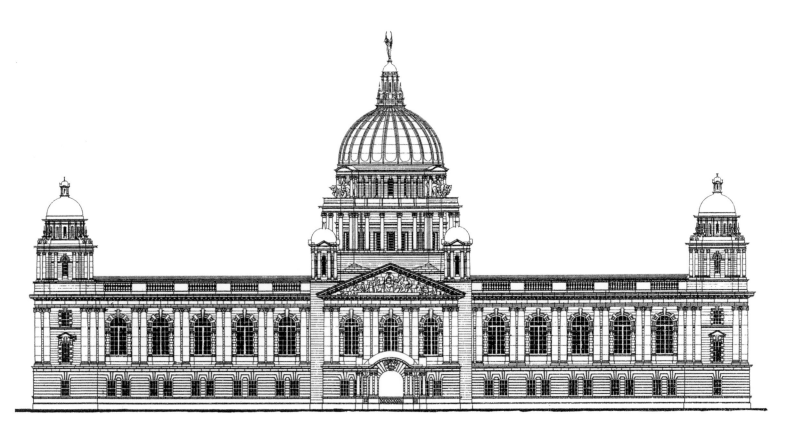

Above: *Front elevation of the winning scheme by E. Thomas & Son, 1897 [from* Building News, *June 1897]*

drawings show considerable improvement. The conditions of the competition have been observed, with trifling exceptions: for example, the competitors do not appear to have adhered to the injunction that their perspective views should be taken from a prescribed spot, and in consequence the authors of numbers 2 and 3 have sent in views taken from a point from which the building in execution could not be seen'.

The winning scheme by E. Thomas & Son had been estimated by its authors at £150,000 exactly, the limit set for the competition, while Stark & Rowntree had estimated theirs at £149,735, and James Miller his at £149,517. These sums had, however, been reckoned by the assessors to be actually nearer £157,000, £166,000, and £174,000 respectively, which supported their view that the scheme of E. Thomas & Son was the best in every way, and so it was recommended for adoption. As the assessors further explained in their confidential report:

'To sum up our opinion, we consider that all the designs may be looked upon as complying with the conditions, [but] that Plan No 1 is decidedly the best, both from its convenience and its directness. Its elevations also gain in dignity what they lack in grandiose effect when compared with the other two, and saying this we are not unmindful of the beauty of detail which characterises Plans No 2 and 3. This combined with the fact that Plan No 1 is, in our opinion, rather less expensive

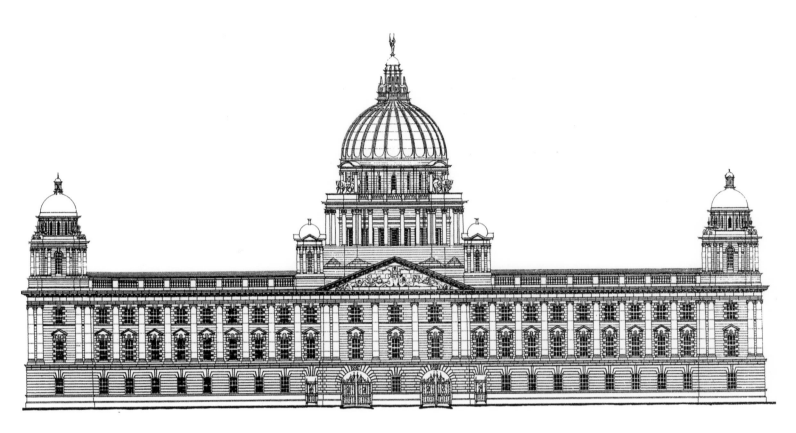

THE WINNING DESIGN

Above: Rear Elevation of the winning scheme by E. Thomas & Son, 1897. [from Building News, *June 1897].*

than either of the other two induces us to recommend it for your adoption'.

The decision of the assessors was accepted at a vote of the City Council on 22 March 1897 and E. Thomas & Son were officially declared the winners. With an optimism that must have already seemed misplaced, if not foolhardy, it was repeated that the cost was not to exceed £150,000. That aspiration was eventually to fall well wide of the mark, for the completed building was finally to cost over £320,000. At least another ambition would eventually come to pass: one of those present, a Councillor Reid, rather prophetically, as we have now come to see, expressed the hope that 'a city hall would be built which would attract tourists from all parts of the world'.[22]

The winning design, which was the work of a young architect, Alfred Brumwell Thomas, the son in the firm of E. Thomas & Son, was an impressive essay in what was known at the time as the Classic Renaissance style, in a particular form of it that has now come to be termed Baroque, or to be more precise, Baroque Classicism.

The choice of a Baroque Revival design as the winner could hardly have reflected Alfred Waterhouse's own personal taste. He had been a committed Gothic Revivalist throughout his career, but he was also an acknowledged master of the large plan, and here he had chosen one of the grandest large-scale designs of the time. Stylistically, the emerging Baroque Revival

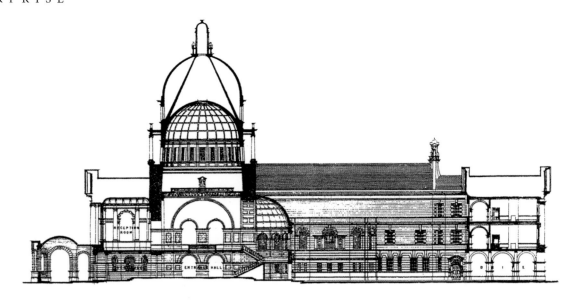

SECTION AA

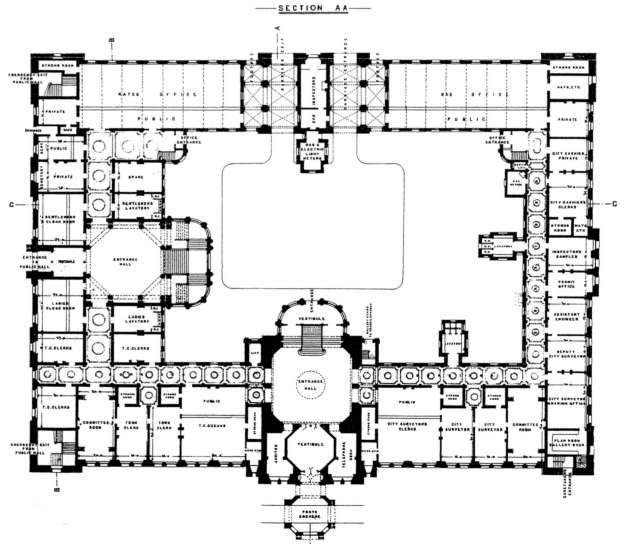

Right: *Ground floor plan and cross section of the winning scheme by E. Thomas & Son, 1897 [from* Building News, *June 1897].*

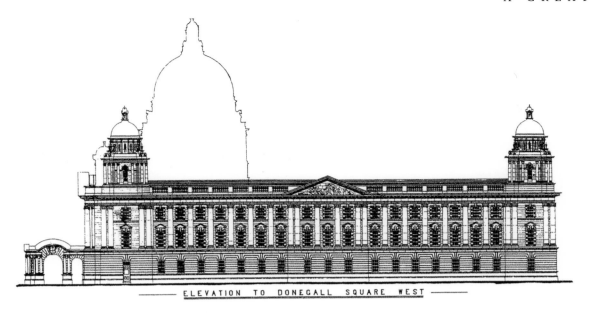

ELEVATION TO DONEGALL SQUARE WEST

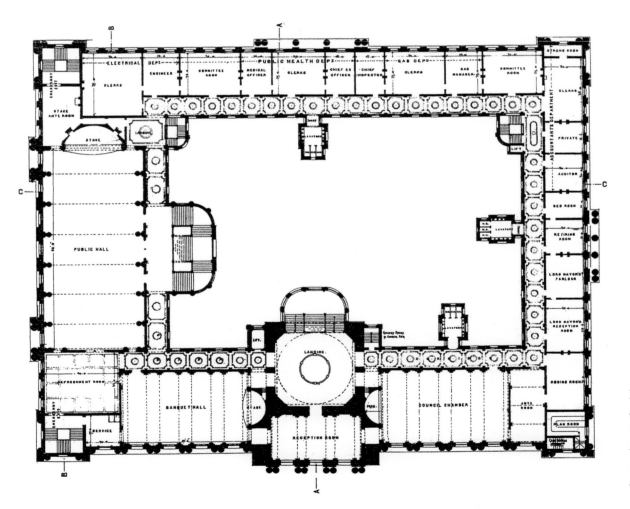

Left: *First floor plan and west elevation of the winning scheme by E. Thomas & Son, 1897 [from* Building News, *June 1897].*

style of the later nineteenth century was felt in some quarters to be rather old fashioned and traditionalist, but it was seen by others as offering the promise of a national style for Great Britain and her empire. Imperial pomp was considered appropriate for a municipal palace such as this, and in any case, Thomas's Baroque Classical forms were moulded around a well organised plan.

The winning drawings were immediately put on public exhibition in Belfast for a month,[23] and later, in June 1897, some of them were published both in the *Building News* and in *The Builder* magazines in London, comprising elevations,

ground and first floor plans and a perspective view.[24] The design was also exhibited at the Royal Academy in 1899, presumably represented by the perspective view, which was later re-published in both *Stone* magazine and *The Irish Builder*, the latter in October 1901.[25]

Thomas's concept was quadrangular in form with an internal courtyard around which were grouped suites of reception and office rooms, in four long wings with two and three-storey outer elevations faced in stonework in a Classical style, utilising columns, central pediments and corner towers with cupolas, the entire composition being dominated by a gigantic central dome.

Below: *Perspective drawing for the City Hall by Graeme-Watt and Tulloch of Belfast, 1896 [from* Building News, *July 1897]*

Left: *Glasgow City Chambers, 1882-90, by William Young [MBR, Belfast]*

This arrangement of a central dome supported by corner towers was a favourite one at the time, and was also adopted, with variations, in the only other published entries for the City Hall, those of Stark & Rowntree, James Miller, and Graeme-Watt and Tulloch.[26]

It was a general arrangement that had been used for some years by a number of other architects elsewhere for buildings of a municipal, public, or especially prestigious type. It can be traced to the Continent as well as in Britain, from the Houses of Parliament in Berlin[27] designed by Paul Wallot in the 1870s, to the Cathedral in Berlin[28] designed by Raschdorff

in the 1890s, and, again with variations, from Glasgow City Chambers[29] by William Young in the 1880s, where there was a tall central tower and cupola rather than an expansive central dome, to various designs for the Victoria and Albert Museum in London in the 1890s such as that by John Belcher. In Thomas's case, as was acknowledged in both *The Builder* and *The Irish Builder*, a great central dome, brought out to near the front of the building block, would perfectly fill the view from Donegall Place where it could be viewed for a distance of over a quarter of a mile.[30]

The sources for Thomas's winning design

Top: *St Peter's Basilica, Rome, by Michelangelo and others: drawing of front elevation, as completed in the early 1600s [from W.J. Anderson,* The Architecture of the Renaissance in Italy, *1927]*

were wide and varied, its forms and details recalling mainly Italian and French Renaissance prototypes, such as the domes of Santa Maria Della Salute in Venice and the Second Church of the Invalides in Paris, as well as more recent German precedent.

For example, the combination of a great dome with flanking cupolaed towers is originally an Italian idea, first seen at St Peter's Basilica in Rome and later at places such as the church of Sant' Agnese in Rome. Similiarly Italian in origin was the motif of a small circular dome rising

Bottom left: *The Church of Santa Maria Della Salute, Venice, 1631-82, by Longhena [from W.J. Anderson,* The Architecture of the Renaissance in Italy, *1927]*

Bottom right: *Second Church of the Invalides, Paris, 1692-1704, by J.H. Mansart [from W.H. Ward,* The Architecture of the Renaissance in France 1495-1830, *1926]*

from a peristyle of columns which was used for the corner turrets, in the manner of Bramante's Tempietto in Rome, itself derived from circular Roman temples. The coupling of columns across the front façade, broken by a central pediment and terminal projections can be seen as French, deriving from part of the Louvre in Paris[31]. An essential inspiration, however, was also English seventeenth and eighteenth-century classicism, with a special debt to London.

Aside from its deep rooted Continental character, and its inescapably Italian cum French

Top: *St. Paul's Cathedral, London, 1675-1710, by Sir Christopher Wren: drawing of front elevation [from W.J. Loftie,* Inigo Jones and Wren, *1893].*

Bottom left: *The Tempietto, Rome, 1502, by Bramante [from W.J. Anderson,* The Architecture of the Renaissance in Italy, *1927]*

Bottom right: *Greenwich Hospital, London, 1696-1715, by Sir Christopher Wren [Author 2006]*

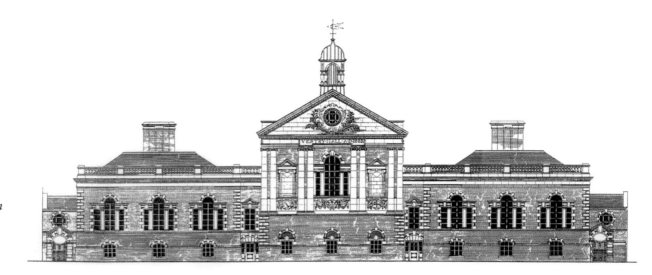

Top: *Chelsea Vestry Hall, 1885-7, by John Brydon [from* The British Architect, *November 1885]*

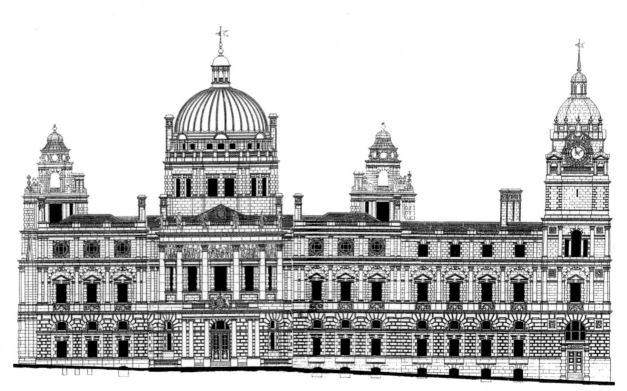

Bottom: *Design for Edinburgh Municipal Buildings by John Brydon, 1886 [from* The Builder, *June 1887]*

appearance, the design was representative of a resurgent interest in English Renaissance architecture, an interest which had been growing steadily since the 1880s and had seen in particular the work of Sir Christopher Wren, architect of such great domed compositions as St Paul's Cathedral and Greenwich Hospital in London, celebrated not only in lectures and publications,[32] but also alluded to in some modern designs and completed buildings which were publicised in the British architectural press. Prominent among these were the influential designs for the Admiralty offices in London[33] by Leeming & Leeming, drawn up in 1884 and eventually built in 1894-5, Chelsea Vestry (later Town) Hall[34] by John Brydon dating from 1885-7, and various unbuilt designs for Edinburgh Municipal Buildings[35] of 1886, such as those by Leeming & Leeming and by John Brydon, all of which Thomas would have known about through illustrations in such journals as *The Builder, The Architect*, and *Building News*. Indeed, the cult of Christopher Wren was gaining such momentum by 1900, particularly among the profession in London, that Thomas's competition-winning design of 1896 would undergo a number of changes in the next few years which would see the intended City Hall take on even more of the characteristics of Wren's architecture than hitherto.

Top: *Detail of St Paul's Cathedral, London, by Sir Christopher Wren, showing a cherub head [Author, 2009]*

Bottom: *St Paul's Cathedral, London, 1675-1710, by Sir Christopher Wren: view from the north-west [from Banister Fletcher,* A History of Architecture, *1896]*

A Dream Palace

THE BUILDING
TAKES SHAPE

In September 1897 tenders were invited for the City Hall, and by December that year the contract to build it had been awarded to the local firm of H & J Martin, whose tender was for £149,864, and in January 1898 site works started.

An early problem even before the outset of construction was the question of how well the ground would bear the enormous weight of the structure, especially that of the dome. The whole building was to stand on soft subsoil, common to a very large area of Belfast.

The only information that Thomas had been able to obtain from the City Surveyor was that there was no established basis for calculation, but that he might count on it that the ground was of 'a yielding disposition'.[36] Thomas therefore decided to drive fourteen-inch thick piles forty feet long every square yard, and sixty feet long under the dome, with a five-feet deep concrete raft seventy-five feet square, in which was embedded a network of steel railway rails bolted to the piles, thus creating an early form of what was later to be called 'reinforced concrete'. These foundations under the dome were to stand the test of time successfully, although some timber piles elsewhere were to require replacing in concrete some years later.[37]

Due to his residing in London, Thomas had felt unable to comply with the Council's desire that he supervise the work once per week. He was only available to visit about once every two months, and so a heavy burden of responsibility was to fall on James Gamble[38] who had been appointed Clerk of Works in November 1897.

His role was to keep things going correctly on a day-to-day basis, but it was to be a difficult job. Early on Gamble encountered problems on site, suspecting that the workmen were sometimes substituting weak concrete mixes for strong, and short piles for long. 'While the Messrs Martin themselves may be anxious to do the right thing it is almost impossible to be up to the tricks of their men' he was reported to have complained to the Council in August 1898.[39]

For their part, the Martins, John and Henry junior, attending a special meeting of the Improvement Committee in October that year, in order to refute these allegations against their men, went on to complain that 'they were being kept back and interfered with, so that the contract at the present rate of progress would take from ten to fifteen years to complete'.[40] Problems may have been exaggerated somewhat on both sides, but a number of short timber piles were discovered during a check in the 1920s, while the contract did end up taking over five more years to complete than originally expected.

Until he was provided with some assistance at the end of August 1898, the Clerk of Works, James Gamble was, however, evidently worn out trying to watch both work on site and preparatory work at the builders' yard at the same time, and attend to correspondence with Thomas. As he explained:

'The "Architect" residing in London throws me to have an amount of correspondence and clerical work that otherwise I would not have. Some of my letters are long and require some thinking out, and sometimes explanatory sketches etc are required with them. You will

Left: *Contract drawing of December 1897 showing a part elevation and part section of the dome and lantern for the City Hall, by Brumwell Thomas [PRONI]*

readily see from what I have said that my opportunities for doing this work are very limited during the day. I have often to do it after working hours, when as a rule I am in very bad form, and with the worry and constant standing on my feet I am sometimes very tired … I think you are hardly aware of the long hours I am on duty here … I come here as a rule at six o'clock a.m. and last week was engaged up to nine o'clock for two nights, and to 8.15, 8.30, and eight o'clock for the three other evenings making an average day of over fourteen hours'.[41]

Over the course of the whole construction

period Gamble was to play an important role, being entrusted with the entire control of the erection of the building and of the various sub-contracts in connection with equipment and general furnishing.

These would eventually include a great diversity of traditional crafts and modern services, from stone carving, marble work, and plasterwork, to electric lighting, lift installation, equipping the buildings with a telephone system, and heating and ventilation by the most modern methods.[42]

Work on site had already been well underway for some time before, on 18th October 1898, the foundation stone of the new building was formally laid by the Lord Lieutenant of Ireland, the Earl Cadogan.[43] The focus of the ceremony, a large block of Portland stone, had arrived at the grounds from England only two days previously, and was suspended from a crane on the platform ready to be placed in its permanent position in the west wall inside the entrance vestibule. Put in the cavity beneath the foundation stone were several articles sealed in an air-tight bottle, including local newspapers, coins, and a description of the intended City Hall, but in addition there was also a phonographic cylinder recording the voices of the Lord Mayor Sir James Henderson, former Lord Mayor William Pirrie, and Sir Samuel Black, the Town Clerk.[44]

Displayed nearby, to enhance the occasion, were full-sized models of a portion of the main exterior cornice and parapet, and a typical capital of the intended building, all fashioned in fibrous plaster.[45]

The actual implements used in the proceedings, a ceremonial trowel and mallet

Below: *Plan of the foundations of the City Hall: a copy made in 1930 by the City Surveyor's Office, traced from the original contract drawing [Belfast City Council].*

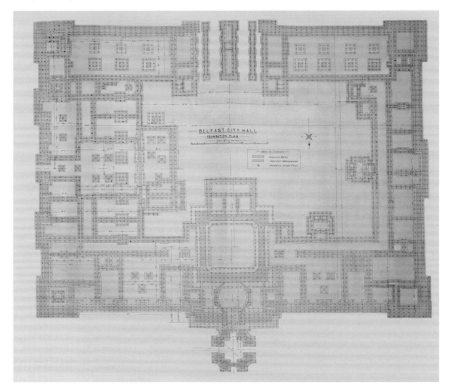

both made of silver and enamel, were designed by the architect Brumwell Thomas in very handsome style,[46] their heraldic devices, so redolent of the Renaissance, together with Baroque cartouches, providing an appropriate foretaste of the ornamental character of the intended new building. The trowel consisted of a simple polished sheet of silver in the shape of an ordinary trowel emblazoned with the Belfast arms, shaped in silver and coloured enamels, to which was attached by scrolls a silver handle decorated with an earl's coronet, three enamelled bosses, Tudor roses and shamrock, and terminating in an imperial crown. The mallet had a silver handle similar to that of the trowel, fixed to the upper surface of a circular ebony block which was overlaid with a silver

Top Left: *Ceremonial trowel, designed by Brumwell Thomas, used in the laying of the foundation stone [Belfast City Council]*

Top Right: *Ceremonial mallet , designed by Brumwell Thomas, used in the laying of the foundation stone [Belfast City Council]*

Bottom: *The laying of the foundation stone on the 18th October 1898 by the Lord Lieutenant of Ireland, Lord Cadogan. The figure in the centre immediately to the left of the stone block may be identified as the architect Alfred Brumwell Thomas. [from James Henderson,* A Record of My Existence as Lord Mayor of Belfast, 1898, 1899]

39

garland depicting the shamrock and rose. Lord Cadogan was formally presented with the trowel by Brumwell Thomas, and with the mallet by John Martin on behalf of the builders, while Lady Cadogan was presented with reproductions in miniature of the two items, but made in gold, commissioned at the suggestion of the Lady Mayoress and presented by her as a memento of the occasion. The miniature trowel, three inches long, was intended to serve as a paper knife and the miniature mallet, two inches long, as a seal. Both the silver and the gold versions were manufactured by the Goldsmiths and Silversmiths Company of Regent Street, London.

However, notwithstanding the formalities of signed contract drawings, an agreed price, and the laying of the foundation stone, a final scheme for the building to be erected was far from settled.

The same month as the foundation stone was laid, there were to be detailed discussions between the architect and the City Council about certain changes that the latter wanted made to the design.

There had been some concern in the Council that, for one thing, the building might not dominate Donegall Square to the desired degree, and indeed Thomas had already taken it on himself to raise the ground floor level about two feet when preparing the contract drawings, so they decided to raise the level about another

Right: *Contract drawing of December 1897 showing long sections for the City Hall, by Brumwell Thomas [Belfast City Council]*

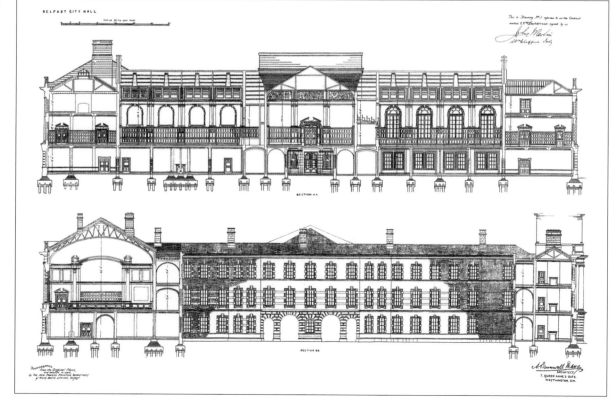

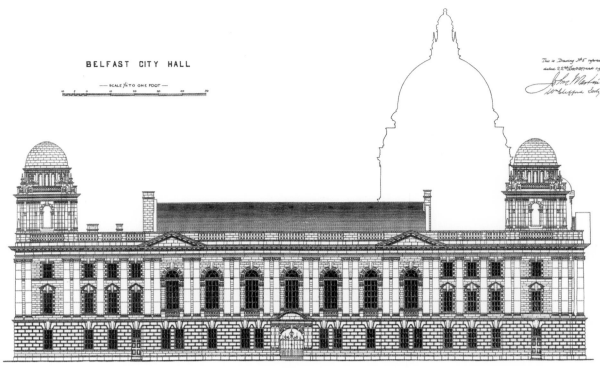

BELFAST CITY HALL

— SCALE ⅛ TO ONE FOOT —

This is Drawing N⁵ referred to in the Contract dated 22ⁿᵈ December 1897 and signed by us

EAST ELEVATION

Left: *Contract drawing of December 1897 showing the east elevation for the City Hall, by Brumwell Thomas [Belfast City Council]*

three feet, which was estimated to cost an extra £3,700.[47]

Bit by bit the overall cost was starting to escalate as other improvements were demanded: substituting stone ashlar for brickwork as a facing to the courtyard elevations and for chimneys, was to cost an extra £3114; raising the overall height of the great dome, an extra £2500; and building stone emergency staircases to the large hall, an extra £1600.

These changes were all at the behest of the Sub-Improvement Committee which had become convinced that such changes were necessary, despite their costliness, for the sake of ensuring that the City Hall would be an 'ornament to the city' for the future and 'a building which they could look upon in years to come as one worthy of their great and improving city'.[48] They recognised that there were things which had been omitted from the original plans in order to curtail expense. As their chairman Alderman Wilson perspicaciously pointed out:

'no doubt had the architects had a

larger margin to work upon they would have given us a finer elevation and a more elegantly proportioned building in the first instance … and your committee are of the opinion that it is better to make good any deficiencies now than that the building should when erected prove unworthy of the city'.[49]

Indeed there were to be many changes between the original winning scheme and the final building. The plan was rearranged in some areas, most notably by first breaking the wall forward along the east side for the length of the great hall, and then later very visibly marking the entrance to that wing by the addition of a projecting porch,[50] but also by squaring off the main stairwells where they bowed into the courtyard, and making the east entrance hall interior compartmented instead of open octagonal in form. Elevationally the most noticeable changes were the raising in height of the front *porte-cochère*; changing the shape of the cupolae on the four corner towers; and changing most of the details of the central dome.

Right: *Contract drawing
of December 1897 showing
the section through the
main entrance hall and
dome for the City Hall, by
Brumwell Thomas [Belfast
City Council]*

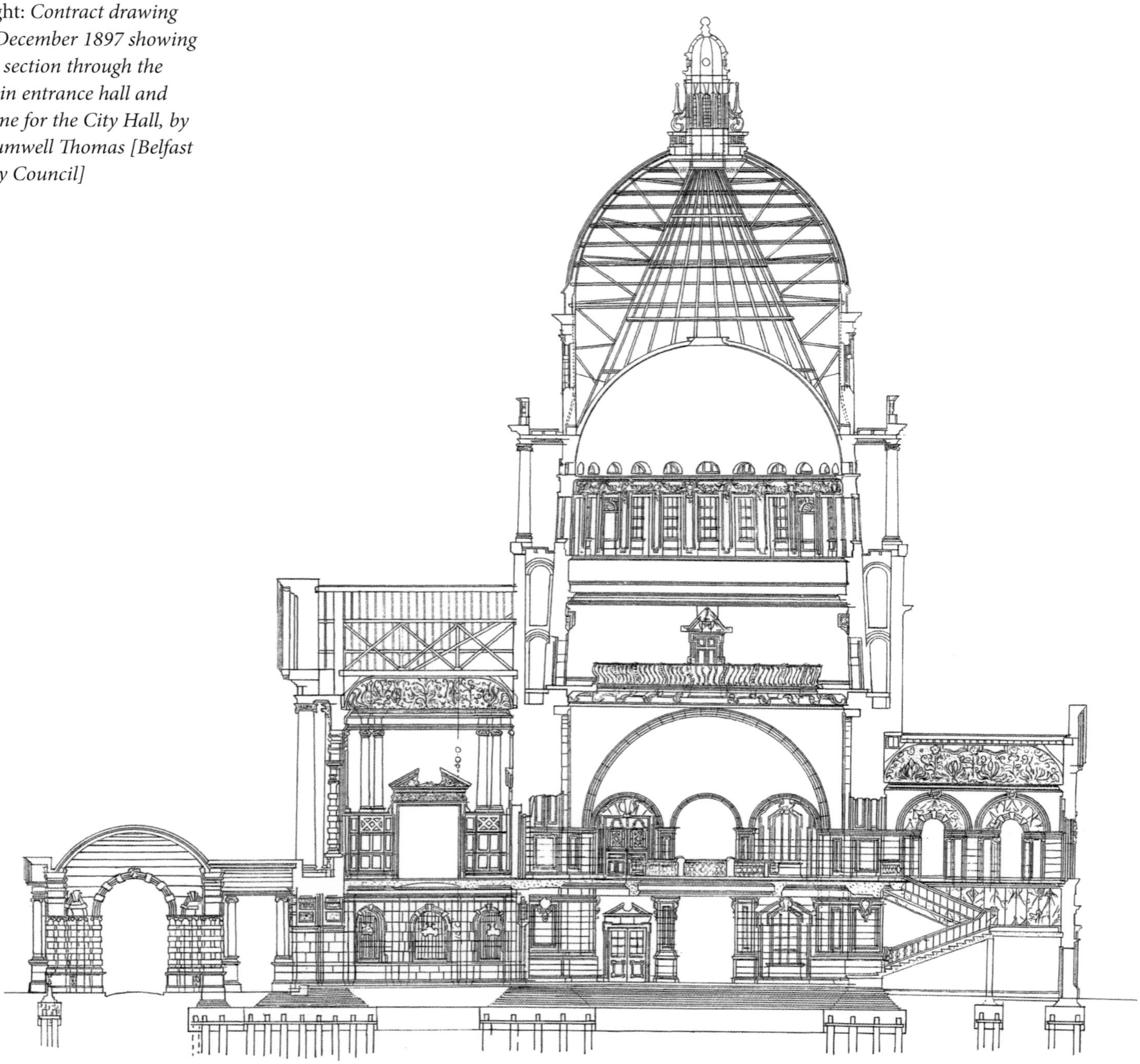

BELFAST
CITY
HALL.
SECTION THRO'
MAIN ENTRANCE
HALL & DOME:

Left: *Section through the main entrance hall and dome for the City Hall showing the details changed and the overall height of the dome increased, by Brumwell Thomas, c1900 [Belfast City Council]*

43

Right: *Section through dome for the City Hall showing the internal decoration scheme and the miniature dome over the 'eye', by Brumwell Thomas, c1901 [PRONI]*

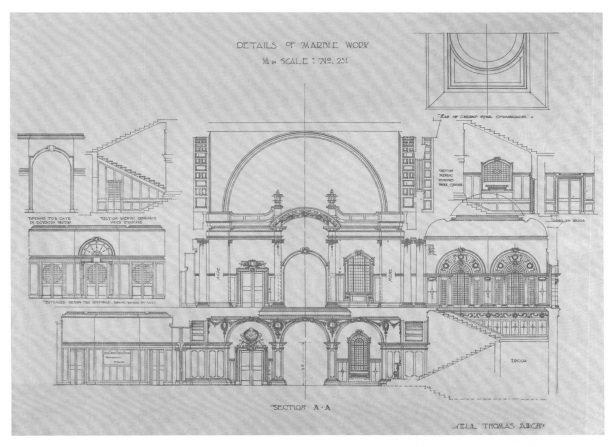

Top: *Cross section through the vestibule, main entrance hall, main staircase and principal first floor landing, showing details of marble work, by Brumwell Thomas, c1901 [PRONI]*

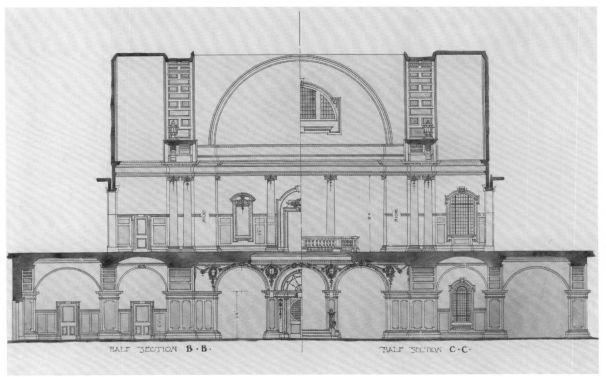

Bottom: *Transverse section through the main entrance hall and principal first floor landing, showing details of marble work, by Brumwell Thomas, c1901 [PRONI]*

Top: *Contract drawing of December 1897 showing the front elevation for the City Hall, by Brumwell Thomas [Belfast City Council]*

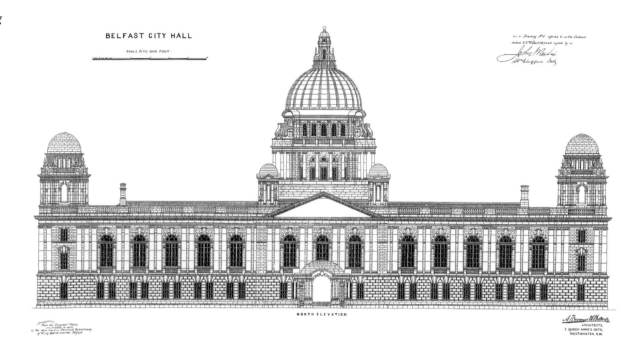

Bottom: *Front elevation for the City Hall, by Brumwell Thomas, c1900, showing the height of the main dome raised and the cupolae of the corner turrets changed to an ogee shape [Belfast City Council]*

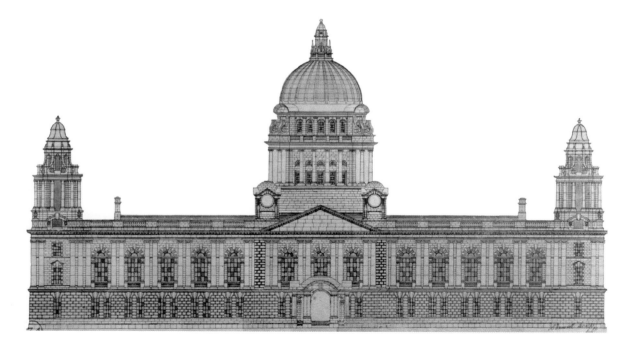

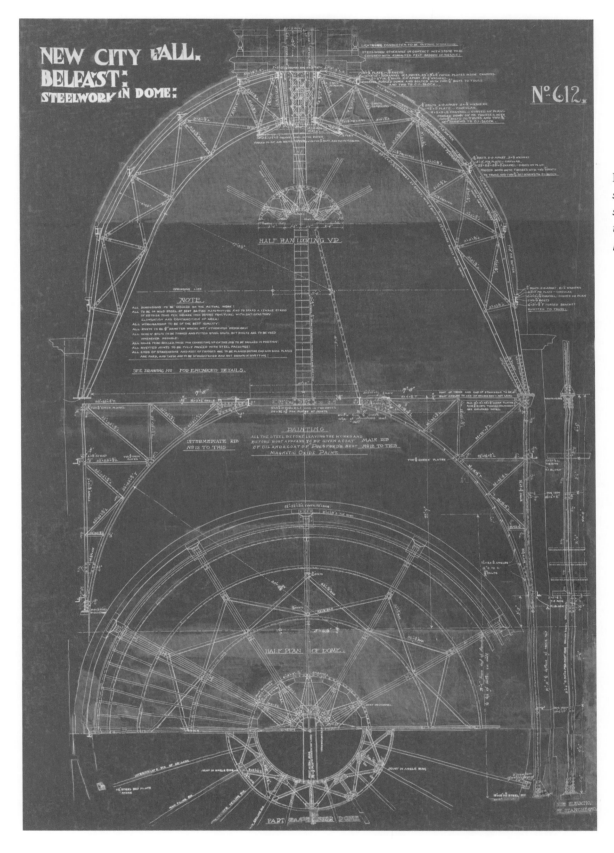

Left: *Blueprint plan and section, c1901, showing the steelwork in the dome of the City Hall as finally built* [PRONI]

In the winning design published in June 1897 the corner towers had hemispherical cupolae, but these were replaced in the contract drawings that December by slightly pointed stone domes, which were shortly afterwards themselves supplanted by hemispherical domes, and eventually, in the finished building, by ogee cupolae based on the western towers of St Paul's Cathedral. In this way the Belfast building was provided with one of the most striking and beautiful features of the entire architectural scheme.

The central dome had rather Germanic looking equine sculptural groups in the winning design. These emerged from the pedimented corner porticoes to the top of the drum, and gigantic figures were recessed in the corner porticoes of the peristyle projecting below. In the contract drawings, however, they were supplanted by comparatively simple large scrolled brackets, which themselves were eventually replaced in the final building by simply sweeping buttress walls.

As the project progressed, Thomas's stylistic homage to the work of Christopher Wren becomes increasingly evident. It is underlined by changes in the corner towers and by the reduction of the drum and peristyle of the central dome to something looking more like those of Wren's Greenwich Hospital. Also, the originally intended octagonal balustrade to the lantern of the great dome was replaced by a circular one, while the semi-circular arched windows to the top of the drum were replaced by rectangular windows, both features derived from St Paul's Cathedral.

Along the way, Thomas provided drawn proposals for a rusticated treatment of the *porte-cochère*, which he eventually left with plain columns; for both two-bay and three-bay versions of the main entrance hall; for ogee heads to internal doorways, eventually left rectangular; and for flat ceilings with coved friezes to main rooms, which he eventually finished with vaulted ceilings and saucer domes, the latter a feature derived from Wren. He also proposed, in 1903, that instead of copper, the great dome should be covered with lead, as St Paul's was, but the Improvement Committee decided that

Right: *Perspective sketch for the east porch of the City Hall, by Brumwell Thomas, c1899 [from The Irish Builder, January 1900].*

he should adhere to the original specification in that particular instance.[51]

Aside from any obvious specific stylistic borrowings from the earlier architect, Thomas, like Wren, seems also to have had the extraordinary aptitude for developing his designs during the actual process of building. Just as Wren's St Paul's, as built, was better than any of his early drawings had shown, so would Thomas's completed City Hall be even better than his winning designs had promised.

When the job started in 1898 it had been anticipated that it would take three and a half years to complete but in fact it was to take eight.

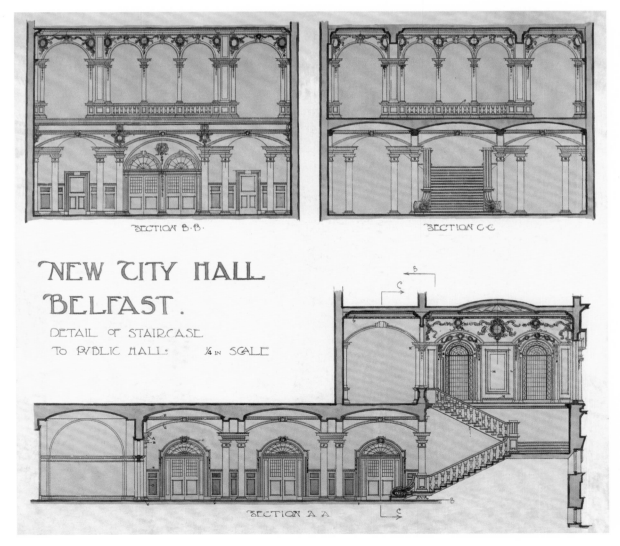

Left: *Sections through the east entrance hall and staircase for the City Hall, by Brumwell Thomas, c1900, showing some details which were eventually changed [PRONI]*

Progress on site was fairly slow, the press noting in July 1900 that the first floor had still not been reached.[52]

By October the next year, however, the underside of the main cornice had been reached, although the roofs had not yet been started, according to the *Irish Builder* magazine which also reported that the architect was at that time, in 1901, laying out schemes of interior decoration before the City Council, and had just received tenders for the marble treatment of the main staircase and the interior of the dome area.[53] The lowest tender for the marble work was £21,681, by Farmer & Brindley of London,[54] a big addition to the overall cost of the building which was now estimated at a quarter of a million pounds. It was a considerable extra but one

which would transform the interior. As Thomas was to recall many years later, this scheme of marble decoration was to be 'the making of the building'.[55]

There were other extras too which were intended to enhance the interior. These included more elaborate plasterwork than had been first specified, as a result of members of the Council being disappointed on viewing the first rather simple finishes that were executed. This was only achieved at an extra cost of £5000 beyond the original of £2000 which had been allowed.

The extras also included a scheme of stained-glass work, for which the Corporation sanctioned the sum of £2500, but only with the approval of a Local Government Board. The increased expense of all the extras had resulted

Right: *The City Hall under construction, c1901-02 [Hogg Collection, Ulster Museum].*

Top: *The City Hall under construction, May 1903 [Hogg Collection, Ulster Museum].*

Bottom: *The City Hall under construction, c1904 [Hogg Collection, Ulster Museum].*

Top: *View down from the whispering gallery showing marble pavings on both ground and first floor [Author, 2009]*

Bottom: *Blueprint plan for setting out of marble pavings of the ground floor vestibule, main entrance hall, and the principal first floor landing, c1900 [PRONI]*

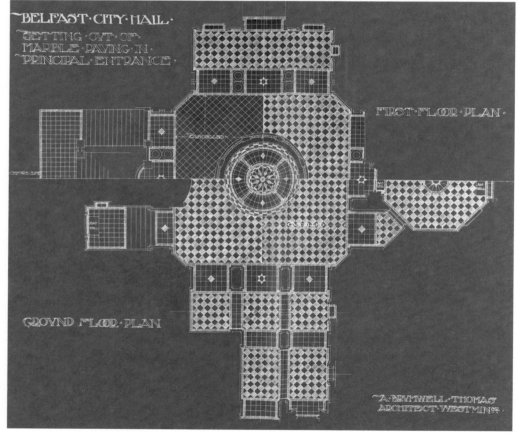

Left: *Unveiling of Queen
Victoria Memorial in
front of the City Hall
in July 1903, with the
King and Queen in the
foreground [Belfast City
Council]*

in a Local Government Board inquiry being set up in 1902, to investigate the spiralling overall cost, followed by another one in 1905.

By March 1903 Thomas was able to report to the Improvement Committee that 'The whole of the structure of the main building is practically complete, except the projecting entrance at ground level', and that 'the structure of the dome is completed to a height of about 50 feet above the level of the main building, or 90 feet above ground level'.[56] The massive bulk of all this was evident, shrouded in scaffolding, when the King and Queen arrived at the site in July that year for

the unveiling of the Queen Victoria Memorial standing in front of the building.

By the beginning of 1905, however, the City Hall was nearly finished, far enough on at that time to be described in the architectural press as 'a great building' and as 'unquestionably the finest public building of recent years in the United Kingdom'.[57]

Finally, by the next year, 1906, ten years after it was first designed, this 'dream palace', as one newspaper correspondent referred to it, was complete.[58]

THE OPENING

The building was formally opened on Wednesday 1st August 1906.[59] It had been expected that the ceremony would be performed by the King, who had previously been in Belfast to unveil the statue of Queen Victoria in the City Hall grounds in 1903, but he was not available this time, and so the honour fell to the Lord Lieutenant of Ireland, the Earl of Aberdeen. It was a wet and windy day as Lord and Lady Aberdeen approached the building at 11.15 that morning to the sound of a royal salute, and passed through a guard of honour by the Royal Inniskilling Fusiliers to be met by the Lord Mayor, Sir Daniel Dixon and the aldermen and councillors awaiting at the *porte-cochère*.

A ceremonial gold key, designed in the style of the Italian Renaissance and made by Gibson & Company of Belfast, was used to open the building through a central folding door between the vestibule and the main entrance hall.

Inside, the architect and the main contractor were briefly presented to the visitors before the entourage moved upstairs to the Council Chamber where, from the dais, the Lord Lieutenant, in a brief speech, with such words as 'may the beauty and grace of the design and execution of this building and its artistic features symbolise and more than symbolise the culture of all that is best in public and private life', declared the City Hall officially open, to an immediate fanfare of trumpets outside in the grounds.[60]

There were about one hundred people in the Council Chamber, but many more elsewhere in the building, dispersed between the reception room, the banqueting hall, and the great hall, about two thousand invitations in all having been issued. The Lord Lieutenant made a short speech in each of these rooms, especially noting in the reception room, with 'great appreciation and interest', as he put it, but also no doubt some amusement, the inscription already confidently placed in position in a memorial window recording that he had been responsible for opening the building.[61]

In the great hall an ode, set to music, was also performed for the visitors. Despite being specially written for the occasion and running

Right: *A drawing of the ceremonial gold key for the official opening of the City Hall [from* The Belfast News-Letter, *August 1906].*

to over twenty verses and choruses there was no mention in the ode of the building itself, or the architectural setting, beyond one reference to 'this august pile, raised as a lasting memorial, reflecting heaven's kind smile', and another to 'Industry, Art, Perseverance' being 'enshrined in each noble arch'.[62] At lunch in the great hall at 1.30 the architect Brumwell Thomas made a brief speech in which he described the building as 'a monument to the character of the people of Belfast' and then went on to pay particular tribute to the craftsmanship involved in the stained-glass and the woodcarving in the building, identifying two shared qualities – 'it was excellent and it was local'.[63] The day concluded with a reception and ball given by

Below: *The stained-glass inscription from a window in the Reception Room of the City Hall recording the official opening [Author, 2009]*

ANNO DNI

1906

The
CITY HALL
was opened
by
His Excellency
The Lord Lieutenant of Ireland,
The Earl of Aberdeen G.C.M.G.

1st August. 1906.
The Rt. Hon. Sir Daniel Dixon Bart MP DL
Lord Mayor.

William Macartney   A Brumwell Thomas
Chairman of Committee.   Architect.

Sir Samuel Black Knt.
Town Clerk.

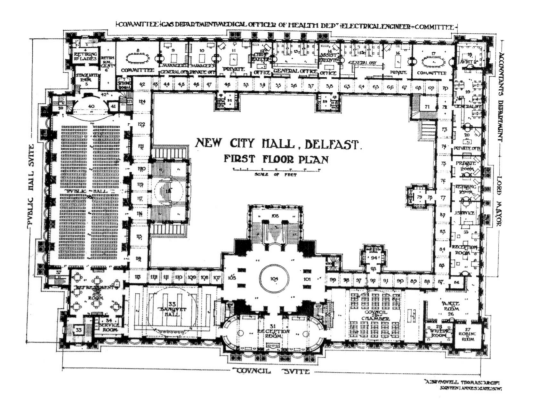

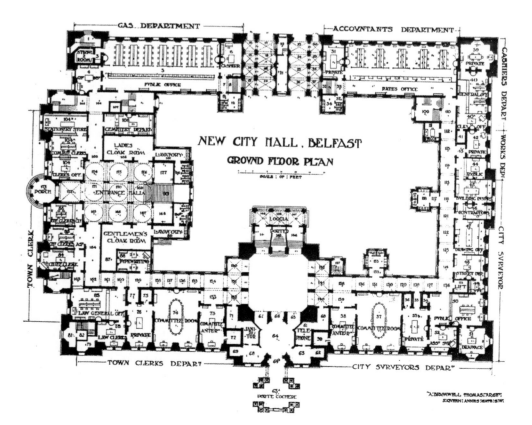

Right: *Ground and first floor plans of Belfast City Hall at the time of opening [from* Architectural Review, *October 1906]*

the Lord Mayor at which the Viceregal party was present. In all, two thousand five hundred guests were invited and the whole of the City Hall thrown open to them to visit.[64]

In connection with the opening of the City Hall an attractive monograph, largely written by the architect, was published by Bairds of Belfast as a souvenir and record containing a general description of the building, and a number of views of the exterior and interior taken by the Belfast photographer, Alexander Hogg. Bound copies of it were formally presented to Lord and Lady Aberdeen at the opening ceremony. It formed the basis of some of the press descriptions of the building at the time of opening, such as the extensive report in the *Belfast News-Letter,* while its photographs were reproduced shortly afterwards in such architectural journals as the Dublin-based *Irish Builder and Engineer* and the English-based *Architectural Review.*[65]

Below: *General view of the City Hall from north-west on the eve of the opening in 1906 [from Baird's 'Monograph of the City Hall', 1906].*

Exterior of the Building

Previous Page: Rear view of the main entrance hall block and great dome, from the courtyard [Author, 2009]

The City Hall as built is a palatial building in a Baroque Classical style characterised on its exterior by long horizontal lines broken by corner towers and a dominant central dome, and faced throughout in Portland stone, the very durable white stone as was used by Wren at St. Pauls; almost thirty thousand tons of it was used.[66] Much of the impact of the building outside is due to its enormous bulk. It is impressive in its dimensions, the principal façades to front and rear extending for 300 feet, with side façades of 230 feet. The height to the parapet is 55 feet while the corner towers are 115 feet tall, and the main dome, with its lantern, rises to a height of 173 feet from the ground.

Not surprisingly, given Thomas's London background, the main elements can be traced to London sources: the neo-Palladian wall treatment of an Ionic order carried on a rusticated ground floor and featuring pedimented breakfronts on each elevation probably comes from Sir William Chambers[67] at Somerset House in the late eighteenth century, with the order changed. Chambers had used the Corinthian order; here Thomas has used an unfluted Roman Ionic order with well modelled angular capitals of the type made popular by the Italian Renaissance architect and writer Vincenzo Scamozzi,[68] in which the scrolls are shown at the sides as well as at the front. The heavily rusticated window surrounds, with alternating large and small blocks, come from James Gibbs,[69] whose use of the motif in the early eighteenth century was so prolific that it has given rise to the term 'Gibbs surround'. The vigorously designed ornamental surrounds to the circular windows in the side and rear pediments probably also come from Gibbs, although there

is something of the feel of John Vardy's Spencer House[70] there too, while Thomas's acknowledged homage to Wren is evident in both the general domed conception and many other details, as well as his choice of stone.

While much of the building's success is due to the high degree of modelling outside, another salient feature is the way the varied exterior elements have been unified by such means as the use of a single order throughout; continuous cornices around the building; balustrading to all four main elevations; and a fine consistency of detailing and finish overall. Each façade is, however, treated differently.

NORTH FAÇADE

The north (or front) façade is mainly two-storeyed, with large public rooms occupying the lofty upper storey above ground floor offices, but with three-storey towers at the ends forming the transition to the three-storey side elevations. Most of the windows are fairly standard rectangular timber sliding-sashes within rusticated stone surrounds. However, the large semi-circular windows of the main public rooms are filled with stained-glass and are set in more elaborate surrounds; these include rusticated Ionic pilasters with pulvinated or cushioned frieze blocks carrying shouldered or lugged hood mouldings with keystones of vigorously carved cartouche form – all being very much a lively mix of details from the repertoire of Wren and Gibbs. The centrepiece of the front façade is the pedimented breakfront containing the reception room on the first floor above the main entrance, with the Council Chamber to

Above: *The north façade of Belfast City Hall photographed on completion in 1906 [Lawrence Collection, NLI]*

the right of it and the banqueting hall to the left. The arrangement of coupled columns, although French in essence, no doubt comes more directly from the portico of St Paul's.

The pediment is adorned by an allegorical sculptural group representing 'Hibernia bearing the torch of knowledge, encouraging and promoting the commerce and arts of the city', designed by Frederick Pomeroy,[71] an important architectural and monumental sculptor from London, and executed by him along with James Winter[72] of Belfast.

In the centre is depicted Hibernia or Erin, a symbolic figure of Ireland wearing a mural crown (that is, one which depicts city walls), with her right hand resting on a harp, the symbol of her nationality, while in her left hand she carries a torch, the symbol of light and advancement. Immediately to her left, as we view it, is Minerva, the goddess of wisdom and of science, attended by Mercury the messenger, the god of commerce, who together take under their protection shipbuilding and navigation as typified by the figures in the left-hand angle of the pediment. Immediately to the right of the central figure stands Liberty awarding the palm branch, signifying victory, to Industry, a female figure offering up a roll of finished linen, while at her feet sits another figure at an Irish spinning wheel, with a seated figure representing 'Design' in the right-hand angle. Completing this somewhat overcrowded scene are two boys in intermediate positions watching the passing events and intended to express the youth and energy of the community.

It is a spirited group, vigorously designed, and characterised by both its technical proficiency, derived from Pomeroy's period of Parisian

Right: *Centrepiece of the north façade photographed on completion in 1906 [Lawrence Collection, NLI]*

Above: *Pediment
of the north façade
[Author, 2006]*

training, and its mannered *contrapposto* effects derived from the Italian Renaissance, which combine to make it a perfect compliment to its architectural setting.

In front of the central main entrance stands a domed *porte-cochère* which seems to have no obvious precedent and appears to have been an entirely original creation by Thomas. In the form of an open pavilion, it comprises a stone-vaulted canopy supported on coupled columns laid out on a square plan, with additional segmental pedimented archways projecting to the sides. It was criticised at the time of opening of the building by a correspondent in the *Irish Builder and Engineer* for interrupting the horizontal sweep of the main front and detracting from the

Left: *Arched window-head in the north façade [Author, 2006]*

Right: *Detail of* porte-cochére *showing a cartouche embellished with the arms of the city* [Author, 2006]

pedimented centre,[73] but on the other hand it can be seen to mark very effectively the location of the otherwise subdued main entrance, as well as playing an important part in the gradual build-up of domed forms which culminates in the great peristylar dome beyond. The original appearance of the *porte-cochère,* and indeed its original integrity as a structure has unfortunately been spoiled by the later covering over of the stone cupola to give the appearance of a copper dome. In its original state it was a little gem of a structure, its baldequin canopy form providing one of the delights of the building outside, while its variation in detail from the main façade, with a pulvinated frieze and delicate wheat-ear decoration on the column shafts, gives promise of further ornamental effects inside the building.

In a transitional position between this *porte-cochère* and the great dome are twin miniature temple-like turrets, which stand immediately behind each end of the central pediment. Stone capped and with diagonally placed coupled columns, these serve no apparent practical purpose but visually support the main dome,

Left: *The* porte-cochère *at the main entrance [from Baird's 'Monograph of the City Hall', 1906]*

Right: *The build-up of domed forms at the centrepiece of the north façade [Author, 2009]*

and provide it with a framing device as viewed from the front, perhaps inspired by elevational drawings of St Paul's and paraphrasing its close-set twin western towers.

The great dome is one of the glories of Edwardian architecture in the British Isles; it is certainly the finest of any period in Ireland. While it clearly continued in the tradition of great Renaissance domes from St Peter's in Rome to St Paul's in London, and the church of the Invalides in Paris, and owes something to each of them, it possesses features which distinguish it from them all. For one thing it is covered in green weathered copper rather than lead. From an almost crag-like base rises a peristyle around the drum which, instead of running right round with an even rhythm, is broken forward at four diagonal corners to create four sets of four columns between tall radiating buttress-porticoes, a very effective arrangement which gives an appearance of great strength and solidity while still retaining a sense of delicacy.

Above the peristyle is a stone-balustraded gallery and attic, again broken by two-tier pedimented flying-buttress-like projections sweeping up to support the dome. The gallery actually passes through the attic projections to reveal them as empty chambers lit by pale green leaded lights in the lunettes whose translucency helps to lighten the visual load of the massive drum when seen from a distance, while the boldly formed dressings of the attic windows, including inaccessible balconette cills, contribute to the vigorous modelling of the overall architectural form. Above it all, the great dome itself is crowned by a volute-scrolled stone copper-cupolaed lantern, a perfect little Baroque

Top: *The stone lantern crowning the great dome [Author, 2006]*

Bottom: *Interior of a portico chamber at gallery level above the peristyle of the great dome [Author, 2006]*

extravaganza in its own right, whose form calls to mind the top-knot in the main dome of the Salute church in Venice.

At each extremity of the main front façade of the building are the corner towers, beautifully proportioned and of tapering profile, contracted but attenuated versions of the great dome and drum. From a square-plan attic on each end bay, lit by segmental arched windows and bedecked by large stone vases, each tower rises like an open temple on a circular plan with convex bays of columns 'in antis' (that is, between piers), framed by coupled columns projecting on four diagonals.[74] Above this stage, flying buttresses, whose open-arched form is not completely visible from ground level, sweep up to a circular open stone lantern surmounted by an ogee copper cupola with a copper urn finial. At the base of these turrets, flanking the segmental arched leaded lights of the outer faces, are cherub heads boldly carved in relief, a motif that comes from the tradition of Wren and Gibbs. [75]

Below: *Detail of a corner tower showing carved cherub heads [Author, 2006]*

Left: *One of the corner towers of the City Hall [Author, 2009]*

EAST FAÇADE

The east façade, as rich in its own way as the north, is partly three-storeyed at the ends, and partly two-storeyed, with the Great Hall, the largest of the public rooms in the building, occupying the twin-pedimented tall upper floor of the central projection, situated over ground floor offices. The 'state' entrance to this wing is marked by a projecting circular porch in the centre of the façade, its form clearly derived from James Gibbs's church of St Mary-le-Strand[76] in London, but here with cherub heads around the frieze outside and a circular border of fruit and foliage on the ceiling inside, all carved in high relief. The other doorways are exits, from

Below: *The east façade of the City Hall [Author, 2006]*

emergency stairways at each end of the great hall and from the stairway in the north-east corner tower, rather than entrances. Bowed balconies to the windows of the Great Hall, similar to those of the north front public rooms, and a central segmental open pediment above the parapet, along with other curvilinear details, add to the overall Baroque effect of this façade.

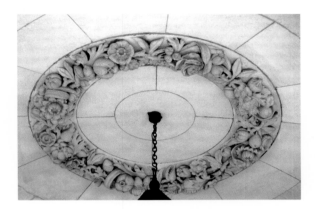

Left: *Detail of the east porch showing ceiling carvings [Author, 2006]*

Below: *The east façade of the City Hall photographed on completion [Welch Collection, Ulster Museum]*

Right: *Detail of the east porch of the City Hall showing a cherub head [Author, 2006]*

Below right: *The church of St. Mary-le-Strand, London, 1714-17, by James Gibbs, showing a circular porch [from James Gibbs,* A Book of Architecture, *1728]*

Below left: *The east porch of the City Hall [from Baird's 'Monograph of the City Hall', 1906]*

SOUTH FAÇADE

The south (or rear) façade is much plainer than the north and east, its three storeys and a basement[77] expressing departmental offices rather than public rooms, with a mainly pilastered treatment to the *piano nobile*, engaged columns being confined to the dominant five- bay breakfront in the centre which contains twin rusticated carriage archways into the courtyard, flanked by pedestrian gateways. A further doorway, at the eastern extremity of this façade and opening directly onto the pavement, gave access to the caretaker's apartment and to retiring rooms at the rear of the Great Hall stage, all on the upper levels. Aside from the corner

Below: *The City Hall from the south-west, showing the south façade to the right* [*Author, 1987*]

Right: *Centrepiece of the south façade [Author, 2006]*

towers which are common to all the elevations, this façade is straightforwardly Classical; it is Baroque only in the vigorously treated carving around the *oeil-de-boeuf* or bull's eye window in the central pediment, which includes a lion's head, and on the keystones of the larger archways, decorated with cherub heads.

Top: *Design for a circular window with a lion's head [from James Gibbs,* A Book of Architecture, *1728]*

Bottom: *Detail of south façade pediment showing a circular window with a carved lion's head [Author, 2006]*

Below: *The west
façade of the City
Hall photographed
on completion
[Welch Collection,
Ulster Museum]*

WEST FAÇADE

The west façade is of similar character to the south and almost identical in treatment except that the centre-piece is of three bays instead of five and contains only windows, with no arched openings in its base. Of three storeys throughout, this wing contains the Lord Mayor's apartments on the first floor, the rest being departmental offices.

THE COURTYARD

The courtyard is approached from the rear of the building by pairs of linked pedestrian footways and carriage driveways, which run through the depth of the south wing, either side of a central porter's lodge. The view through these stone cross-vaulted passages, with their chunkily rusticated Ionic columns engaged with square piers, seems like 'a glimpse into the courtyard of an Italian palace' as a contemporary put it at the time.[78] The decision during the course of the contract to construct the courtyard in Portland stone instead of brickwork was a happy one from an artistic point of view and gives some cohesion to an asymmetrical space with very variegated parts which display an interesting range of door and window openings.

On axis with the driveway, beyond a modern circular fountain, is the three-bay main stairway projection, which has a series of finely detailed Palladian windows above boldly rusticated Ionic

Below: *The courtyard looking north-east showing staircase projections [from Baird's 'Monograph of the City Hall', 1906]*

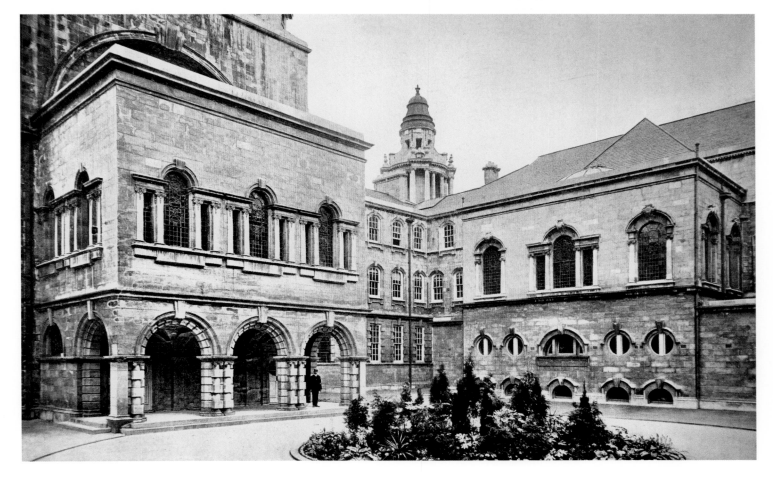

Right: *A rear driveway looking into the courtyard beyond [from Baird's 'Monograph of the City Hall', 1906]*

Left: *Rear of the main entrance hall block and great dome as viewed from the courtyard [from Baird's 'Monograph of the City Hall', 1906]*

Right: Elevational drawing of openings within a pedestrian passage in the south wing of the courtyard, by Brumwell Thomas c1900 [PRONI]

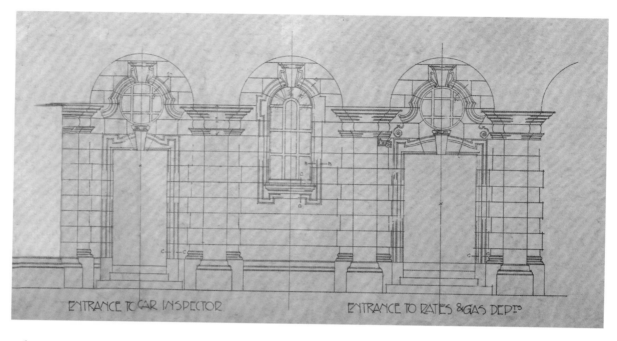

ENTRANCE TO CAR INSPECTOR   ENTRANCE TO RATES &GAS DEPTS

columns. It is set forward from the looming and largely solid-walled mass of the entrance hall block which carries the drum of the great dome towering above and provides overall an unexpectedly powerful sight when seen at such comparatively close quarters as the courtyard.

The fountain in the courtyard was newly introduced in 2009 to replace a small circular flower garden, an original feature of Thomas's which lasted for over a century before being swept away with the resultant loss of the contrast which its blooms and greenery made with the sombre masses of stone. Off to one side, in almost uncomfortably close proximity to the main stairway projection, is the eastern stairway projection where as many as five different window types, including Diocletian, Palladian, and *oeil-de-boeuf*, are crammed together on its main face, producing a very quaint effect.

The main three-storey elevations all around the courtyard, meanwhile, have mostly rectangular sashed windows in rusticated surrounds on the ground floor, and mostly segmental arched sashes in shouldered surrounds, with aprons, on the upper storeys, the main wall planes being punctuated at intervals by tall narrow stairwells and toilet stacks which rise through three floors. There are, however, handsome rusticated and triangular pedimented doorways at the southern end of both the east and west wings, the former with its pediment rising up into the Diocletian window above, a little High Renaissance Mannerist touch that echoes on a small scale a similar arrangement by James Gibbs at the Fellows' Building, King's College, Cambridge.

Elsewhere within the comparatively hidden elevations of the courtyard area Thomas gave further rein to a more inventive streak in detailing than he could permit himself on the more public outer faces of the building where he was consciously conforming to a particular historic tradition. The doorway type used in the loggia below the main stairway, and in the wall alongside it, has a rectangular architrave superimposed on a pair of rusticated Ionic pilasters leaving only half a capital visible to each side, an idiosyncrasy that was repeated in the wall arcading within the pedestrian passages in the south wing, and one which owes more to the Mannerist strain of the Italian Renaissance than to mainstream English classicism.

The wavy moulded heads to doorways within those pedestrian passages, with scalloped and

Left: *Doorway at the southern end of the east wing in the courtyard [Author, 2006]*

Bottom left: *Doorway in the loggia below the main stairway on the north side of the courtyard [Author, 2006]*

Bottom right: *Window within a pedestrian passage in the south wing of the courtyard [Author, 2006]*

Right: *Doorway within a pedestrian passage in the south wing of the courtyard [Author, 2006]*

Above: *The south wing, as viewed from the courtyard [Author, 2006]*

Right: *Drain-pipe hopper in the courtyard, modelled with a cherub's head and dated 1904 [Author, 2009]*

scrolled ogee pediments above, make us wish that he had broken free from his deference to English neo-Palladianism more often and given us more of the Baroque flourishes of which he was capable. One last feature to note in the courtyard elevations are the hoppers on the drain pipes, moulded in lead and inscribed '1904', one of the very few dates to be displayed anywhere in the original phase of building, with the underside of each modelled with a cherub's head, presumably the work of the Bromsgrove Guild of Worcester.[79]

INTERIOR OF THE BUILDING

The exuberance of the exterior of the City Hall is carried through to the interior in a fine series of public rooms and circulation spaces, with some lavish use of imported marbles and a superb quality of material and workmanship in stained-glass, carved woodwork and modelled plasterwork.

VESTIBULE

The main entrance through the *porte-cochère* leads into an octagonal vestibule in which the decorative treatment in plasterwork and Italian marbles gives a foretaste of the main circulation areas beyond. The plaster ceiling has a circular moulding of running flower and fruit design, while the floor is laid in black and white marble chequerwork paving of diagonal pattern with a central star in an octagon, and the walls are lined with rectangular panels of mottled multi-hued breccia marble on a black marble plinth, and a cornice above of white blue-veined Italian

Pavonazzo marble.[80] Pavonazzo is also used for the engaged unfluted Doric columns of the doorway in the south wall leading to the main entrance hall, and for the cherub's head keystone on the open fanlight above it.

The vestibule is notable now for the later addition of an exquisite marble sculptural group to the memory of Frederick Richard Chichester, Earl of Belfast, who had died of consumption at the early age of 26 in 1853. This is an outstanding

example of Victorian sculpture, considered by some the most beautiful monument of its type in Ireland. This masterpiece of the Belfast-born but London-domiciled sculptor Patrick MacDowell depicts the Earl lying on his death-bed being mourned by his mother[81]. Originally housed in Belfast Castle Chapel, it was removed for safekeeping in 1979 and given to the Ulster Museum which placed it here on permanent loan in 1981. Facing it and set in the west wall is the inscribed foundation stone which was laid with great ceremony on 18th October 1898.

MAIN ENTRANCE HALL
AND STAIRCASE

Beyond the vestibule is the splendid main entrance hall, its walls and piers lined with similar marbles to the vestibule, and its floor also laid in black and white marble chequerwork paving, mainly of diagonal pattern, but set with a large radiating centrepiece, inspired no doubt by a similar treatment at St Paul's Cathedral.

Semi-circular arcaded openings are ranged round all four sides, leading to saucer-domed lobby areas to left and right, and thence to office corridors, with a magnificent grand staircase beyond to the rear. In a stroke of genius by Thomas, the flat ceiling of the central area of this entrance hall opens up through a large circular light-well to allow a stupendous view

Below: Main entrance hall showing circular light-well in ceiling [Author, 2009]

Far left: *View through circular light-well of the main entrance hall towards the great dome [Author, 2009]*

Left: *Decorative plasterwork in main entrance hall area [Author, 2009]*

to the inside of the great dome poised 100 feet above. This adds a touch of drama to the already considerable sense of space experienced on first entering the hall.

Palm fronds, garlands of fruit, and cherub heads in decorative plaster of excellent quality, the work of George Rome & Co, of Glasgow,[82] ornament the spandrels and frieze of the central arches, while off to the sides are fine marble doorcases to the two main front rooms, embellished with open pediments and ornate carved cartouches.

Adding to this scene of decorative splendour are the original pendant bronze light fittings of curvilinear design, encircling the large opening in the centre of the ceiling, and marble dressed windows with carved cherub head keystones and colourful stained-glass medallions depicting a sailing ship, emblematic of Belfast, in the twin rear entrance passages flanking the main staircase.

As one reporter commented when the building first opened:

'This hall has nothing to do with the workaday world of red brick suburbs and unsightly smoke-blackened factories. It exists for beauty only – beauty of space and proportion, form, and colour, designed with a skill that leaves one blinking in mute admiration, carried out with a sovereign disregard for cost very rare in these utilitarian days'.[83]

A later addition of art-historical interest to this main entrance hall is the First World War memorial stained-glass window to the North Irish Horse, depicting a standing figure of a youthful warrior clad in golden armour, with upraised sword in his right hand and a helmet in his left hand, and a small vignette of Saint George

Right: *Marble doorcase to a front room off main entrance hall [Author, 2009]*

Far Right: *First World War memorial window commemorating the North Irish Horse, by Ward & Partners, 1925 [Author, 2006]*

and the dragon, St George being the patron saint of Cavalry; it was designed and made by Ward and Partners of Belfast, and unveiled by the Earl of Shaftsbury on 30th April 1925.

The grand staircase to the rear of the main entrance hall is one of the most notable features in the entire building. It is constructed of the same Italian marbles as the rest of the ground floor hall, with the addition of Carrara,[84] also from Italy, which is used for the large scrolling

Below: *Main staircase looking from the half-landing to first-floor around 1906 [Welch Collection, Ulster Museum]*

Above: *Main entrance hall [from Baird's
'Monograph of the City Hall', 1906]*

Above: *Main or grand staircase at the base [from
Baird's 'Monograph of the City Hall', 1906]*

brackets at the base of the stairway and for the actual steps themselves, the bottom three of which bow outwards over the floor of the hallway. Of double return arrangement, the stairway has an impressive array of seven three-light arched windows, of a type known as 'Palladian' or 'Venetian', ranged round the three side walls, all dressed in highly veined Pavonazzo marble, and filled with leaded lights of matching delicacy,

with a domed ceiling overhead finely modelled in plasterwork and supporting an impressive central bronze electrolier, which, like the marble keystones around the walls is decorated with cherubs' heads.

The stained-glass of the windows was made by Ward and Partners of Belfast. It is largely of heraldic design, with the arms of Belfast in the centre, but also includes portraits of King

Below: Main staircase showing windows and marble panelling at the half-landing [Author, 2009]

Top: *Stained-glass medallion in a window of a rear entrance passage off the main entrance hall [Author, 2009]*

Bottom left: *The base of the main stairway [Author, 2009]*

Bottom right: *Bronze electrolier above the main staircase [Author, 2009]*

95

Above: *View from the main entrance hall through the circular light-well towards the John Luke mural on the principal first floor landing [Author, 2009]*

Right: *Detail of a stained-glass window of main staircase showing a portrait of King Edward VII by Ward and Partners, 1906 [Author, 2009]*

Edward VII and Queen Alexandra framed in Classical canopies, and records various stages in the history of Belfast.[85] This spans the period from granting of the original charter by King James I in April 1613, to 1899 when it became a County Borough, and includes the names of the first municipal councillors. Turned balustrading of Pavonazzo marble, intricately carved details of cartouches and wheat ear garlands on the newel posts, and cherub head keystones to the window arches sustain the effect of a 'marble wonderland', as one contemporary termed the main entrance area.[86]

Left: *Main
staircase at half-
landing with
views of ground
and first floors,
including the
Earl of Belfast
statue in its
initial position
in the main
entrance hall in
1906 [Lawrence
Collection, NLI]*

Below: *Principal first floor landing looking toward the colonnaded screen of the main stairway [from Baird's 'Monograph of the City Hall', 1906]*

PRINCIPAL FIRST FLOOR LANDING

At the top of the main stairway lies the principal landing on the first floor.[87] With its large circular Pavonazzo marble-balustraded well in the centre of the floor, opening to view the entrance hall below, and a colonnade of Ionic columns around all four sides, with four great arches supporting the drum, and the coffered dome itself, soaring above the whispering gallery, this is one of the grandest architectural spaces in Ireland. Powerfully monumental in its domed form, but enhanced by the Baroque

Left: *Principal first floor landing
showing the light-well in the floor
and the Earl of Belfast statue
within the colonnaded screen
[Author, 1987]*

Right: *Principal first floor landing under the great dome [from Baird's 'Monograph of the City Hall', 1906]*

Left: *Bronze statue of the Earl of Belfast by Patrick MacDowell, dating from 1855, on the principal first floor landing [by courtesy of Chris Hill and Belfast City Council]*

Right: *Lateral view of principal first floor landing, from east to west, showing pedimented archways [Lawrence Collection, NLI]*

INTERIOR OF THE BUILDING

imagination of Thomas to allow a view from one floor to another, it is a majestic and wonderfully scenic concept enriched by fine materials.[88]

Similar marbles as are used in the entrance hall and stairway are also used here, but with the addition of Cipollino for the columns of the colonnade and their responding pilasters.[89] These large monolithic shafts, whose colour runs from translucent green to blue, were brought from the island of Euboea off the coast of Greece. Cipollino marble, characterised by wave-like markings produced when it was cut 'across the bed', was highly regarded in antiquity by the

Left: *Plasterwork in the principal first floor landing on a spandrel supporting the drum of the great dome [Author, 2009]*

Romans, but had fallen out of use, only for its best source to be rediscovered after some years of searching by William Brindley,[90] the principal of the London firm of Farmer and Brindley which supplied all the marbles for the City Hall. It stands out here, even in this rich setting, as an element of very special quality.

The principal landing overall is a wonderfully orchestrated space with nicely modulated surface effects, as in the open pedimented marble niches in the north wall, the bulbous projections of the entablature and blocking course of the

Far left: *Plasterwork on an angled corner of the principal first floor landing [Author, 2009]*

103

Above: *Lunette in rear wall of principal first floor landing [Author, 2009]*

colonnades on the angled corners beneath the four great arches, and the equally Baroque, but more monumental, open-pedimented archways leading to left and right, a form repeated from the sides of the *porte-cochère* on the main entrance front of the building, embellished now with carved marble cherub heads and vases.[91] Original decorative elements which add to the overall richness of this interior are the heraldic

glass depicting the arms of James I in the semi-circular lunette occupying the main archway to the rear of the landing above the colonnaded screen, and the elaborate modelled plasterwork that embellishes its frame, and especially also enriches the spandrels supporting the drum of the dome where Mannerist masks appear.

The mural painting in the tympanum of the main arch to the front wall of the landing is a

Far left: *Stained-glass window by Daniel Braniff commemorating Lady McCullagh [Author, 2009]*

Left: *Stained-glass window by Daniel Braniff commemorating Sir Crawford McCullagh [Author, 2009]*

Above: *Detail of the mural on the front wall of the principal first floor landing painted by John Luke in 1951-2 [Author, 2009]*

later addition, painted by the Belfast artist John Luke[92] in 1951. Commissioned by C.E.M.A. (the Council for the Encouragement of Music and the Arts, which was the forerunner to the Arts Council of Northern Ireland) to mark the 1951 Festival of Britain, and unveiled in May 1952, it illustrates the formal foundation of the city with the reading of the town's first charter in 1613, by a figure in Jacobean costume who may be intended to represent Sir Arthur Chichester, in a setting depicting some of its later buildings and industries. Its highly formalised style was typical of John Luke's work.

Another important later art work on the principal landing is the very fine bronze statue of the Earl of Belfast by Patrick MacDowell, at the head of the staircase, originally erected in 1855 in the roadway in front of the Royal Belfast Academical Institution at College Square East, then moved to the old Town Hall in Victoria Street in 1875 and from there to the Public Library on Royal Avenue in 1888, and finally brought here to the City Hall to be placed in the ground floor entrance hall[93] in 1906 before eventually being moved to its present position.

Other later, or added, art works on the principal landing are four marble busts along the north side, representing Sir James Henderson by Frederick Pomeroy of London, dated 1921;[94] Lord Carson by Leonard Merrifield of London, dated 1940;[95] Sir James Emerson Tennent by Patrick MacDowell, dating from the early to mid-nineteenth century; and the Rt Hon John C. White by Sydney March of London, dated 1922. There are also three stained-glass windows of art-historical interest, namely a First World War memorial to the 36th (Ulster) Division, depicting figures of 'Valour' and 'Truth' and an inset panel showing a portrait of King George V, by Ward and Partners, unveiled on 26 June 1920,[96] on the east side, and a much later pair of excellent quality on the south side commemorating a former mayor Sir Crawford McCullagh and his wife, depicting historic events of their period, including the war-time bombing of the City Hall itself, in a series of small-scale figurative panels, by Daniel Braniff of Belfast.

Right: *First World War memorial stained-glass window commemorating the Ulster Division, by Ward & Partners, 1920 [Author, 2009]*

Above: *Peristyle window in the drum below the great dome, depicting 'Leo', made by Campbell Brothers [Author, 2009]*

WHISPERING GALLERY AND GREAT DOME

Above the four main arches on the principal landing is the whispering gallery, whose very name[97] even has echoes of St Paul's Cathedral, with its circular balustrade cantilevered out on ornamented brackets at the base of the drum which carries the dome, and a range of peristyle windows higher up in the drum, filled with excellently drawn and richly coloured stained-glass medallions, designed by John Bewsey for Brumwell Thomas and executed by Campbell Brothers of Belfast, depicting the signs of the zodiac, alternating with symbols of the ship and bell which form quarters of the Belfast arms.[98]

Covering it all is a great domed ceiling, elaborately panelled and ornamented in plaster, while above the open central eye of this dome is a secondary miniature dome, an entirely interior element, carried on a circular colonnade of eight Ionic columns around the eye and encased in a circular chamber. Suspended from this uppermost point and capable of being lowered as required, by a system of pulleys, is a large bronze electrolier. This is a 2009 replacement for the original, long since removed, which consisted of 100 lights arranged in clusters and was ornamented with laurel wreaths cast in bronze, repeating a leading motif of both the peristyle windows and the coffered dome.

The great dome of the City Hall, which is the most striking feature of the building both internally and externally, is actually of double construction, with an outer dome covered in copper and an inner one constructed of steel with decorative plaster attached to it. This inner dome

Left: *Interior of the great dome viewed from the Whispering Gallery [Author, 2009]*

Below: *View down from the eye of the great dome through the Whispering Gallery and the light-well in the principal first floor landing to the main entrance hall [Author, 2009]*

is the one which one sees above the principal landing. In this arrangement of two layers of large domes, one is carefully scaled to be in proportion to the rest of the interior, while the other is raised much higher so as to be in proportion to the overall exterior of the building. In this way it provides a sufficiently dominant effect outside, which the inner dome alone could not have done.

By using this double dome construction, Thomas was following on from Sir Christopher Wren at St Paul's Cathedral except that the structural methods were different. Wren had to carry the weight of his stone lantern at the top of the outer dome on a brick core which had timber trussing around it, while Thomas could turn to the more modern expedient of trussed steel ribs.

Left: *The Whispering Gallery [Author, 2006]*

Top: *Bronze electrolier hanging in the great dome in 1906 [from Baird's 'Monograph of the City Hall', 1906]*

Bottom left: *View along inside face of the outer dome showing the steel ribs [Author, 2009]*

Bottom right: *Simplified half-sectional drawing through the great dome [Belfast City Council]*

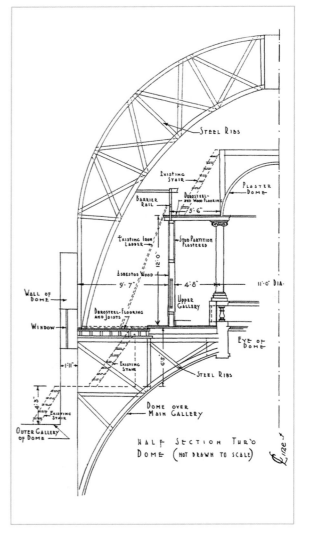

Left: *The Whispering Gallery and great dome, over the mural by John Luke [Author, 2006]*

Right: *Miniature dome above the eye of the great dome [Author, 2009]*

A pair of completely enclosed staircases, one at each end of the first floor landing, on the north side, lead up to the whispering gallery on the inside of the drum, the peristyle passage on the outside of the drum and the gallery passage above it, and eventually give access to the area between the two domes, which contains the passage around the eye, and thence to the lantern outside, all of which are closed to the public.

Top: *View into the miniature dome above the eye of the great dome [Author, 2009]*

Bottom left: *Cartoon, or full-sized preparatory drawing, for a peristyle window depicting the bell symbol from the Belfast Arms [Belfast City Council]*

Bottom right: *View down from the eye of the great dome to the Whispering Gallery [Author, 2009]*

Right: *Stained-glass window in the Reception Room, incorporating the Royal Arms, by Ward & Partners [Author, 2009]*

FIRST FLOOR ROOMS

To left and right of the principal landing, through lugged archways marked by carved marble cherub head keystones, are corridors leading past public rooms ranged across the front of the building, to the Great Hall along the east side, a private suite of rooms for the use of the Lord Mayor along the west side, and an office wing to the south. En suite to the front of the building are the reception room, the banqueting hall and the Council Chamber, all entered from the principal landing through rectangular marble dressed doorways containing panelled double-doors of oak with ocular glazing.

RECEPTION ROOM

The reception room, directly across the landing from the main staircase, is a fine room in Classical taste, exedrae-ended in plan, with a barrel-vaulted ceiling supported on fluted Ionic columns with entablature blocks, and terminating at either end with panelled semi-domes. Walls are panelled in wainscot oak of plain appearance with more ornamentally treated woodwork to the doorcases in the three interior walls, which have scrolling brackets, and palm fronds and wreaths in the open pediments,

Opposite page: *The Reception Room in 1906 [from Baird's 'Monograph of the City Hall', 1906]*

Right: *A stained-glass window by Ward & Partners in the Council Chamber depicting the Belfast Arms [Author, 2009]*

carved by Purdy and Millard of Belfast. A nice decorative quality is also apparent elsewhere, as in the richly moulded plaster details of a Carolean character in the ceiling, both in the borders around the panels of the main vault and in the open-work grilles of the air vents in the cross vaults; the original pendant light fittings in bronze; and the three stained-glass windows by Ward and Partners containing elaborate Renaissance canopies, with amorini or cherubs, surmounted by heraldic designs, showing the Royal arms of Edward VII in the centre window and the arms of the city, inscribed with its motto *'Pro Tanto Quid Retribuamus'* in the windows to either side.

COUNCIL CHAMBER

The Council Chamber, to the left of the principal landing and also connecting with the reception room, is the administrative heart of the building. A nicely proportioned room, it is oak wainscoted and galleried, with a central domed ceiling which is richly decorated in plaster, and flanked by vaulted end bays which each contain a pair of ornamentally treated air vents displaying the monogram 'BC' for Belfast Corporation. As in the dome of the main first floor landing, but on a smaller scale, the domed ceiling here has an open oculus or eye at the apex for ventilation purposes, with a miniature peristyle of Tuscan colonnettes visible above it, through which a large bronze electrolier is suspended. Elsewhere, smaller pendant bronze light fittings hang from the ceiling surfaces. The seating for the members of the Council is laid

Left: *The Council Chamber in 1906 [from Baird's 'Monograph of the City Hall', 1906]*

Right: *Lord Mayor's Dais in the Council Chamber with woodcarvings by Purdy and Millard [from Baird's 'Monograph of the City Hall', 1906]*

out on the English 'House of Commons' model with a central gangway, but the general feel is of a Wren church interior, especially so as the focal point, the oak screen and Lord Mayor's chair on a dais, both excellently carved in the manner of Grinling Gibbons, with an ornamentally treated desk in front, has the appearance and feel of a reredos behind a communion table. The carvings on these furnishings, and on the members' seats, the large public balcony and smaller press balcony fronts, as well as the wainscot frieze around the walls was by Purdy and Millard of Belfast, who were responsible for all the ornamental woodcarvings in the building. So intricate are the designs of the three pierced and carved panels on the screen that they alone occupied a number of sculptors for months.

Other original decorative elements of note are the lions' heads in plaster on the square piers around the walls, and the heraldic designs in the four stained-glass windows. These latter, representing the Royal arms, the Belfast arms, and the arms of Lord Dufferin and Lord Londonderry, were made by Ward and Partners. The original covering for members' seats and other chairs, of green morocco leather stamped with the city arms in gold has, however, been replaced.

Left: *Detail of plasterwork in the Council Chamber showing a lion's head [Author, 2006]*

Right: *Ceiling of the Council Chamber showing the ventilation eye at the apex [Author, 2006]*

Below left: *Detail of plasterwork around the dais in the Banqueting Hall [Author, 2009]*

Below right: *The eye in the dome of the Banqueting Hall ceiling [Author 2009]*

BANQUETING HALL

The banqueting hall, to the right of the principal landing and also connecting with the reception room, corresponds in size and shape to the Council Chamber, but without the galleries. It also has similar Austrian oak wainscoting, heraldic stained-glass windows, again by Ward and Partners, original electroliers, and plasterwork, except in the saucer dome of the ceiling, which is ribbed and so has a different range of details, although it also has a miniature Tuscan cupola above the ventilating eye. One later change from the original features in the room is the replacement of the original ornamentally treated plasterwork air vents in the vaulted end bays of the ceiling by simple modern grilles. The focal point in this room is the ornate little dais at one end, to accommodate musicians, embellished with very well modelled plasterwork cherubs. The stained-glass windows display the Royal arms, the Belfast arms, and the arms of Lord Donegall and Lord Shaftsbury.

Left: *The Banqueting Hall in 1906 [from Baird's 'Monograph of the City Hall', 1906]*

Right: *The Great Hall looking toward the gallery, photographed in 1911 [Hogg Collection, Ulster Museum]*

GREAT HALL

Separated from the banqueting hall by what was originally an oak panelled ante-chamber, and occupying almost the whole of the east wing of the building on the first floor, is the Great Hall. Impressive in its size, 120 feet long by 57 feet wide, with a stage at one end and a gallery at the other, it has a segmental vaulted ceiling rising from fluted and coupled Corinthian columns with entablature blocks. As is the case in the reception room, these columns are actually decorative rather than structural, being of hollow timber construction and added solely for the sake of a palatial appearance.

This room was severely damaged by a German air-raid in May 1941 when its roof and ceiling and most of its architectural features were destroyed, but it was rebuilt in 1952, unfortunately however, omitting most of the plasterwork mouldings of the ceiling and failing to replace accurately a number of other plasterwork details.[99] The most notable loss in plasterwork, which was not replicated in the 1952 restoration, was the pair of large kneeling figures, which appear to have been modelled in such high relief as to be almost 'in the round', placed at each extremity of the arch over the stage. They were replaced by smaller less heroically conceived figures modelled by H.H. Martyn & Co of Cheltenham,[100] a firm which had had a share of the stone carving contracts at the City Hall when first built. Another notable loss in the war-time bombing was the series of original electroliers, with lanterns forming part of the design; these were eventually replaced in the year 2000 by new pendant lights that come near to the original form but fail to reproduce it.

Bottom: *War damage to the Great Hall in 1941 [from* Bombs on Belfast, *1941, courtesy of the Belfast Telegraph]*

Right: Stained-glass window by Ward & Partners in the Great Hall depicting Queen Victoria [Author, 2006]

Far right: Detail of the Donegal carpet supplied for the Great Hall in 1912 [from Some Historic Donegal Carpets, 1912]

Despite the war-time damage, however, the original seven stained-glass windows, made by Ward and Partners, have remained intact, having been removed for safe-keeping at the outbreak of war in 1939 – to avoid the force of any bombs that might have hit the shipyards to the east of the city centre – and then returned from storage and re-installed when the hall was rebuilt. They depict portraits of sovereigns who had visited Belfast, namely King William III, Queen Victoria, and King Edward VII, in heavily garlanded tabernacles, as well as shields of the four provinces of Ireland – Ulster, Munster, Leinster and Connaught – each window bordered by leafy surrounds of pomegranates, wreaths, and heraldic motifs.[101] Now missing however, is the great Turkish style Donegal carpet, measuring 107 feet by 46 feet 6 inches and weighing two tons five cwts – the biggest Donegal carpet ever made – which was supplied for this room in 1912.[102]

Left: *Detail of a stained-glass window by Ward & Partners in the Great Hall depicting a shield representing 'Ulster'* [Author, 2009]

Right: *The east staircase in 1906 [from Baird's 'Monograph of the City Hall', 1906]*

Top: *Stained-glass window by Ward & Partners in the east staircase depicting symbols from the Belfast Arms [Author, 2009]*

EAST STAIRCASE AND EAST ENTRANCE HALL

Outside the Great Hall, and off the east corridor, through an arcaded Ionic screen of columns and piers is the east staircase, of similar general form to the main staircase, with a double-return layout and a domed ceiling, and also lit by seven windows, but differing from it in finish and detail. Less magnificent overall, being constructed of fibrous plaster rather than coloured marbles, and with only one Palladian window, the rest being single-lights, it is still very impressive with highly ornate modelled plasterwork details to the upper walls, a large

Bottom: *Ceiling of the east staircase [Author, 2009]*

Right: *First floor landing to the Great Hall [from Baird's 'Monograph of the City Hall', 1906]*

Top: *First floor landing to the Great Hall with the arcaded screen to the east staircase [Author 2009]*

Bottom: *East entrance hall in 1906 [from Baird's 'Monograph of the City Hall', 1906]*

Right: *The bronze memorial to the Young Citizen Volunteers on the half-landing of the east staircase, by Leonard Merrifield, 1924 [Author, 2009]*

original bronze electrolier suspended through the eye of the ribbed dome ceiling, whose decorative scheme extends to the first floor landing, and original heraldic stained-glass medallions made by Ward and Partners. These represent the Royal Arms and the shields of Belfast, Ulster and Ireland. The small bronze soldier on a pedestal of Portland stone standing on the half-landing is a later addition, a First World War memorial to the Young Citizen Volunteers, the 14th Battalion of the Royal Irish Rifles, by Leonard Merrifield in 1924. It represents the figure of a rifleman in fighting kit giving the signal with his rifle, "No enemy in sight'.[103]

The east staircase leads down to the east entrance hall on the ground floor below the great hall, connecting it with the east porch and providing the main access to the great hall from the exterior of the building on gala occasions. This entrance hall has simply treated surfaces but an interesting spatial arrangement of flat saucer-domed compartments marked off by segmental arches on coupled columns, using an unfluted Roman Doric order in one of Thomas's few departures from the Ionic. The columns and ceilings, along with their ornamental details, were all constructed of fibrous plaster, the columns being given from the start a very delicately painted finish to simulate marble, while the flooring was originally laid in mosaic with borders of stylised flower heads around the central area.

Left: *Half-landing of the east staircase [Author, 2006]*

MINOR ROOMS

Top: *An office corridor in 1906 [from Baird's 'Monograph of the City Hall', 1906]*

Elsewhere in the building the minor rooms, mainly departmental and administrative offices, are generally of plain finish and character, although some committee rooms and the mayoral suite have oak wainscoting, ornamental plasterwork friezes and ceilings, and original bronze light fittings. The main committee rooms, on the ground floor off the main entrance hall, also have impressive columned and pedimented oak fireplace surrounds, and contain original furniture, all designed by Thomas, testimony to both his versatility as an architect and his ability to control all aspects of detail throughout the building[104]. The office corridors are lined with pedimented doorways in oak and plain mosaic floors with decorative borders.

Bottom: *The Lord Mayor's Reception Room prior to furnishing in 1906 [from Baird's 'Monograph of the City Hall', 1906]*

Top: *A committee room in 1906 [from Baird's 'Monograph of the City Hall', 1906]*

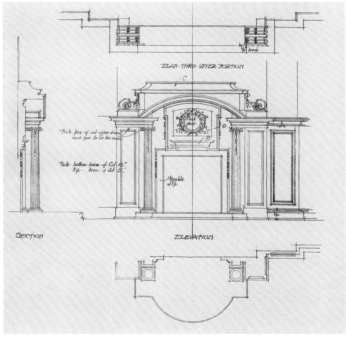

Bottom left: *Drawing for a fireplace in a committee room by Brumwell Thomas, c1900 [Belfast City Council]*

Bottom right: *Fireplace in a committee room [Author, 2006]*

THE GROUNDS

At the time of the opening of the City Hall in 1906 the grounds surrounding the building were laid out in the form of a public garden in which had already been placed a number of monuments. The first two of these had each been carefully boarded up for protection after their initial erection until heavy construction work in front of the building had been completed and they could be officially unveiled.

The general layout of the grounds consisted of lawns sub-divided by mainly circular and slightly curving paths, with a circular driveway leading up to the *porte-cochère*, and shrub-like plantings along the paths, much as had already been indicated by Thomas in his early perspective of the winning scheme that was published in June 1897. The detailed treatment of flower beds and shrubs, however, was arranged by the City Council's superintendent of parks, Charles McKimm.[105]

In addition to the circular driveway through the *porte-cochère* and the notional intention of having a circular fountain within the circle as shown on his perspective drawing, Thomas had gone on, in the block plan of his contract drawings of December 1897, to show a wide gateway at each of the four corners of the site, as well as narrow pedestrian paths flanking each

Right: *View from the north-east overlooking the City Hall grounds in 1906 [Hogg Collection, Ulster Museum]*

138

side of the rear of the building, with linking paths and driveways skirting each side. The later articulation of the east elevation including the partial projection of the east entrance porch, as well as deliberations over the siting of monuments within the grounds, however, led to a change of thought on the overall layout.

A revised arrangement as depicted in a 'general site and garden plan' of 1905, shows two more broad circles to the front portion of the site, one at each corner either side of the central circular driveway, with a crescent shaped driveway from the eastern boundary on axis with the east porch, and a circular pathway occupying the west part of the grounds. These latter were

shown linked by pedestrian paths both to rear pedestrian gateways and to the front corner circles. Monuments were shown blocked in on the four circles, and in two intervening spaces, in a notional suggestion for siting of the first six monuments to be erected, some already in position and some yet to be determined.

The most important of the monuments already set up in the grounds at the time of opening in 1906, still in its original position in front of the *porte-cochère*, and echoing to some extent the statue of Queen Anne in front of St. Paul's Cathedral in London, but much closer to the building and thus of more dominant presence, was the Queen Victoria Memorial by

Above: *View from the north-west overlooking the City Hall grounds in July 1906 [Hogg Collection, Ulster Museum]*

139

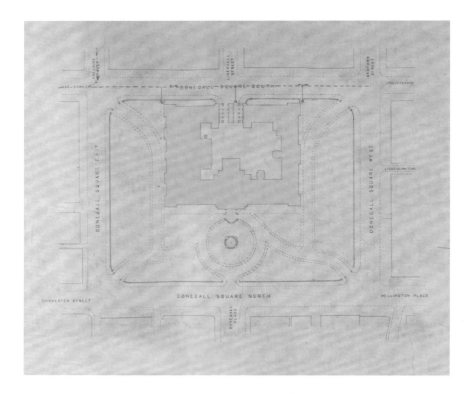

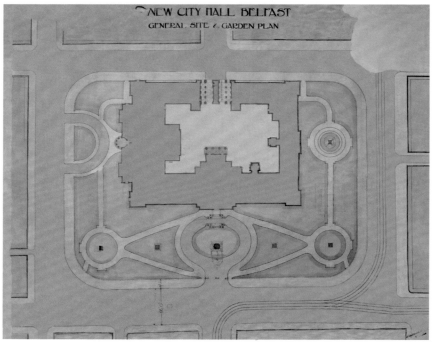

Top: *Contract drawing of December 1897 by Edward Thomas & Son showing the block plan for the City Hall with the intended layout of the grounds [PRONI]*

Bottom: *'General Site & Garden Plan' of 1905 by Brumwell Thomas showing a revised arrangement for the grounds [Belfast City Council]*

the sculptor Thomas Brock of London.[106] Brock was the leading figure in 'official' sculpture in Britain at the time and much in demand for sculptural portraits of the Queen. He had designed her coinage effigy in 1892 and was to start work on the models for her memorial outside Buckingham Palace in 1901, the year he finished the Belfast work.

The monument here consists of a statue of the Queen carved in white 'Sicilian' marble, which actually comes from Carrara in Tuscany and was used extensively in Britain for decorative and monumental purposes. On either side of the pedestal are bronze figures denoting shipbuilding and spinning, and to the rear a small bronze figure of a child reading, personifying education. The Queen is represented in royal robes holding the orb in her left hand and the sceptre in her right, while across her chest is the ribbon of the garter, with the skirt of her dress shown as embroidered with the rose, shamrock, and thistle. The monument was paid for by public subscription, limited to one shilling per person, organised by the *Belfast News-Letter* in 1896 to commemorate the Queen's Diamond Jubilee, and thus the dates '1837-1897' which appear on a large bronze cartouche at the front, and also the inscription on the pedestal – 'From my heart I thank my beloved people; may God bless them' – which was part of her Diamond Jubilee message to her subjects. Designed by Brock in 1897, when a sketch model was exhibited in Belfast, the work was completed by 1901, but there then followed a delay in setting it up as the question of a site had not been settled. Two alternative sites had been discussed, one in front of Queen's College (later Queen's University), and the other in

Below: *The Queen Victoria Memorial by Thomas Brock, 1897-1901 [Author, 2006]*

Above: *The Queen Victoria Memorial on unveiling day in July 1903 with the miniature model of the memorial in silver displayed on the table in front [by courtesy of Alun Evans]*

Left: *Rear view of the Queen Victoria Memorial showing the bronze figure of a child reading [Author, 2006]*

141

Right: *Statue of Sir Edward Harland by Thomas Brock, 1903 [Author, 2009]*

front of the unfinished City Hall. Eventually the present site was decided on and the monument erected in 1903. The pedestal was set up in March that year followed by the statue itself in April. It was then carefully boarded up until it was unveiled on 27th July by the late Queen's son King Edward VII.[107] "The ceremony formed a pleasant interlude in the midst of the building work, at a time when important decisions hung in the balance" recalled Brumwell Thomas many years later.[108] Thomas had, incidentally, been formally introduced to the King on the occasion of this unveiling in 1903,[109] while the King was presented with a miniature copy of the statue in silver by Sir James Henderson the proprietor of the *Belfast News-Letter* and first Lord Mayor of Belfast.

Although the main statue itself was much admired – it was described by the King as the best he had yet seen of Queen Victoria – its siting came in for some criticism at the time,[110] and the complaint was repeated some years later when the grounds were being rearranged,[111] because it was too near the building and centrally placed, therefore blocking out the view of the main entrance on an axial approach.

Just prior to that prestigious Royal occasion in 1903 had been the unveiling, on 23rd June that year, of the statue in white marble of Sir Edward Harland, Bart, MP, who had done so much to build up the prosperity of the city through the development of its shipbuilding industry as head of the firm of Harland and Wolff. Competent but conventional, this, the first statue to be erected in the grounds, was also the work of Thomas Brock, and was unveiled by the Earl of Glasgow, President of the Institute of Naval Architects. At

Opposite bottom:
The four figures on the bronze frieze around the pedestal of the Royal Irish Rifles Memorial representing 'War', 'Victory', 'Death' and 'Fame' [Author 2006]

that time it stood just to the east of the Queen's statue, but was later moved further eastwards to its present position.

To the east of the Harland statue in 1906, situated in the centre of a circular lawn in the north-east corner of the grounds, and also in line with the Queen Victoria Memorial, was the monument erected to the memory of the officers and men of the Royal Irish Rifles who died in the South African War of 1899-1902. Of unusual form, it comprises a bronze rifleman on a base consisting of a rough-hewn granite rock supported by a tapering pedestal of smooth granite with a mechanistically treated core, and a bronze frieze decorated at the four corners by

Right: *Royal Irish Rifles Memorial in its present position in the east garden, with the Titanic Memorial in the background to the right and the Pirrie Memorial to the left [Author, 2006]*

Below: *Royal Irish Rifles Memorial of 1905 by Sydney March shown in its original location in the north-east corner of the grounds [Hogg Collection, Ulster Museum]*

Right: *The Dufferin Memorial from the rear [Author, 1986]*

Far right: *Model for the Dufferin Memorial by Frederick Pomeroy and Brumwell Thomas as exhibited at the Royal Academy in 1906 [from* Academy Architecture, *1906]*

figures representing, War, Victory, Death and Fame, and by a symbolic design of harp and shamrocks, crowned with a wreath of laurel, on one of the panels. Modelled by the sculptor Sydney March of London and cast by Elkington & Co. in 1905, it was unveiled on the 6th October that year by Lord Grenfell, Commander of the Forces in Ireland.[112] It was later moved a considerable distance southwards to its present central position in the east garden, on axis with the east entrance to the City Hall.

The fourth of the original group of monuments set up in the grounds during the course of building the City Hall, and the most ambitious of them all, was the Dufferin Memorial commemorating Frederick Temple, the Marquess of Dufferin and Ava, one of the greatest diplomats of his day, who had been both Governor General of Canada and Viceroy of India. It comprises a bronze figure of the Marquess depicted standing in the robes of the Order of St Patrick beneath a towering stone canopy which is surmounted by a bronze winged figure of Fame, with bronze supporting allegorical figures below representing Canada and India, and was the joint work of the sculptor Frederick Pomeroy and the architect Brumwell Thomas.

The latter was responsible, at the invitation of Pomeroy, for designing the delightful 'four-poster' canopy in Portland stone, whose Baroque Classical treatment with segmental arches and open triangular pediments, and use of Thomas's favoured Ionic order, harmonises so well with the City Hall itself. The monument was designed in 1902, took Pomeroy three years to complete, and was unveiled by the Marquis of Londonderry on 8th June 1906.[113] Originally considered for a position to the west of the Queen Victoria Memorial, to balance the Harland statue on the other side, it was clearly too grand to play that merely supporting role, and so it was set up in splendid isolation in the centre of the large lawn to the west side of the City Hall, as suggested by Pomeroy, on axis with the pedimented breakfront and encircled by a pedestrian path. It was later moved westward to a position near the boundary of the site to make way for the Garden of Remembrance in the 1920s.

The original landscaping of the City Hall grounds by McKimm had a mixed reception at the time, with conflicting views on its garden-like character and its visual effect on the building itself. "The appearance of the building is greatly enhanced by the artistic and garden-like character of its surroundings" was the comment of the *Belfast News-Letter* at the time of opening in 1906,[114] and shortly afterwards they also referred to McKimm's original plan for the grounds as having laid the foundations for what would eventually be "an extremely pleasing piece of decorative work".[115] The local architect and historian Robert Magill Young seemed to concur with this view of the grounds when he later remarked that "the margins are tastefully laid out in flower and shrubbery in a very picturesque and beautiful way".[116]

A contrary viewpoint was, however, expressed by the *Irish Builder and Engineer's* reporter at the time of opening who criticised the "fussiness" of

Right: *Statue of Sir James Haslett by Frederick Pomeroy, 1907 [Author, 2009]*

was a viewpoint shared by the journal's editor who further criticised the "meandering walks, amidst indiscriminate patches of grass lawn, which disfigure the surrounding ground" adding further that "the walks are beneath criticism, and it is doubtful that the architect could have been consulted in reference thereto".[118]

Whether or not consulted on the details of the layout, Thomas himself appears to have been initially happy enough with McKimm's treatment of the grounds and its contribution to the overall setting of his building, remarking, for instance, that 'the added charm of a flower garden bordering the principal public street brings a sense of restfulness and repose seldom attained in a great commercial city'. [119]

Later however, as McKimm's plantings became overgrown in the years that followed, Thomas may have had some misgivings about the matter, as he was to recommend a fundamental rearrangement of the grounds when called on to attend to other matters in the 1920s.

In the decade or so after the official opening of the City Hall the grounds acquired three more monuments. The first was the statue of Sir James Haslett, a former mayor in the 1880s at the time the idea of a city hall was conceived, who died in 1905. It was the work of Frederick Pomeroy, sculpted in 1907 and unveiled in 1909. Similar in character to the Harland statue, with which it was clearly intended to harmonize, it was originally erected to the west of the Queen Victoria Memorial, on a foundation pad which had been set out for it as early as 1906 as can be seen in early photographs of the completed City Hall. Later, in the 1920s, it was moved to its present position to the east of the Queen Victoria Memorial.

the grounds and its ensuing "confusion of flowers and shrubs and sweeping paths, discounting the richness of the building, where simplicity and rest are needed to contrast it", adding that "In a few years the rusticated and severe under storey will be hidden, and the balance of the architectural composition consequently destroyed".[117] It

Top: *Statue of Sir Daniel Dixon by Hamo Thorneycroft, 1909-10 [Author, 2006]*

Then followed the bronze statue of Sir Daniel Dixon, Lord Mayor when the building was opened, who died in 1907. It was unveiled in 1910 and was the work of the sculptor Hamo Thorneycroft, RA. The boldly realistic figure of the main subject dates from 1909, with bronze bas-relief panels on the granite pedestal representing 'Shipping', 'Belfast', and 'Science, Progress, and Education', completed in the following year, 1910. This statute was originally set up within the large circular bed in the north-west corner of the grounds, thereby completing the original set of five monuments evenly distributed across the front of the building, but later was moved in the 1920s.

The last monument to be fitted into the early landscaping layout of the grounds was the statue to Robert McMordie, Lord Mayor from 1910 to 1914. A return to conventionality in marble, and unfortunately rather lacking in spark, it was the work of Pomeroy in 1917, and was unveiled in 1919. Its original position was to the west side of the City Hall, to the rear of the Dixon statue and on axis with the Dufferin Memorial and facing

Left: *The three bronze bas-relief panels by Hamo Thorneycroft representing 'Shipping', 'Belfast', and 'Science, Progress and Education', on the pedestal of the statue of Sir Daniel Dixon [Author, 2006]*

Right: *Statue of Robert McMordie by Frederick Pomeroy, 1917* [Author, 2006]

Below: *Plan for the rearrangement of the grounds by Brumwell Thomas, 1924* [Belfast *City Council*]

BELFAST CITY HALL
SUGGESTED ARRANGEMENT OF
GATES, ENCLOSURE & GARDENS

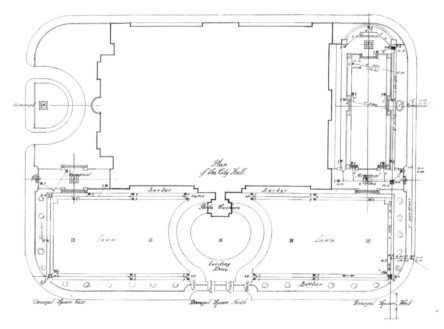

west like the latter,[120] but it was relocated to its present position in the 1920s.

Early in 1924 Thomas drew up a scheme for the rearrangement of the grounds with the idea of providing an improved setting for the City Hall.[121] It called for moving most of the statues; building terraces to each side in line with the front of the building, which would be flanked by balustrades, each terrace to be approached from front and back by steps, and each to contain a memorial; laying out a border of shrubs or flowers around the outer edge of the entire front area and removing the large circular footpaths at the front corners to create broad expanses of smooth lawn flanking the central circular driveway; erecting gates at the main entrance driveway and at the two front corners of the north boundary; and laying out a Garden of Remembrance in the area to the west of the building to contain the intended city war memorial.

Due to differences of opinion between Thomas and the Corporation over the lack of a formal contractual agreement at the time, the execution of his scheme was entrusted to others, namely the City Surveyor, assisted by the Superintendent of Parks, and not all of Thomas's suggestions were carried out at the time – the original laurel hedge around the boundary of the site which he wanted to see removed, was instead retained until recently – while some aspects of detailed layout and design, which were already undergoing revision by him, were also changed. A design in an early sketch plan showing broad seats at each end of the Garden of Remembrance, flanked by pairs of lions and statues on pedestals, was for example, superseded by the eventual arrangement of simple steps.[122]

The Garden of Remembrance as finally

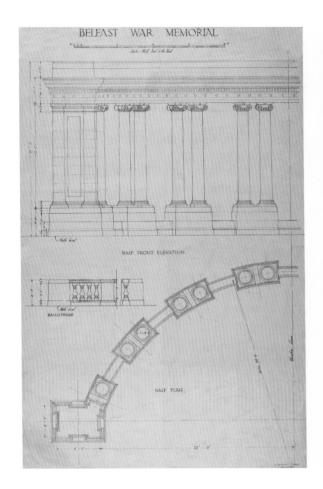

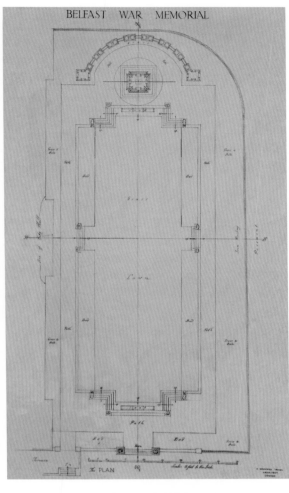

Top left: *Half-plan and half-front elevation of the curved colonnade for the Belfast War Memorial by Brumwell Thomas [PRONI]*

Top right: *Plan for the Garden of Remembrance and War Memorial by Brumwell Thomas [Belfast City Council]*

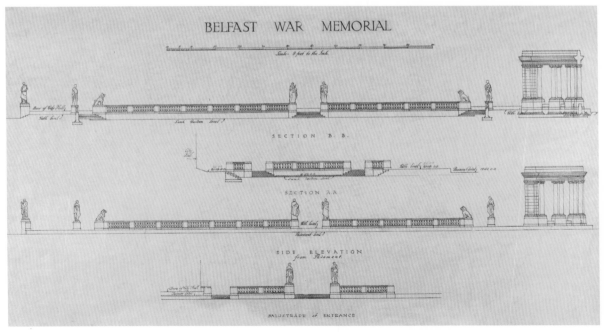

Left: *Elevational drawings for the balustrades and colonnade of the Garden of Remembrance and War Memorial as proposed by Brumwell Thomas [PRONI]*

laid out in the mid-to-late 1920s comprised a balustraded area running along the west side of the City Hall, approached from the north by a wide pathway leading to a paved walk around the periphery of a sunken lawn with a broad flight of steps down to the lawn at the north end, a pair of smaller central steps mid-way along the east and west sides, and a set of broad bowed steps at the southern end leading to the war memorial. By the early 1930s the broad expanse of lawn was divided into four sections by a cruciform arrangement of paths, and by the 1990s most of

the grass had been replaced by a new pattern of paving.[123] The war memorial itself comprises a Portland stone cenotaph, some thirty feet high, standing in front of a curved colonnade of paired plain shafts with Greek 'Tower of the Winds' capitals, terminating at either end in square piers and pilasters, all set on a stepped stylobate or platform. The cenotaph – a monument erected to the dead who are buried elsewhere – takes the form of an elaborate stele or vertical stone, with pilastered faces, carved laurel wreaths to the sides and a garland to the front. The group

Right: *Garden of Remembrance as first laid out in 1929 [Welch Collection, Ulster Museum]*

was designed by Thomas in 1924, constructed in 1925-27, the long delay being caused partly by difficulties in obtaining the required stone, and unveiled by Field Marshall The Viscount Allenby on Armistice Day, 11th November 1929. The builders were W.J. Campbell and Son and the stone carving and inscriptions were by Purdy and Millard.[124] More neo-Classical in feel than Renaissance Revival, the war memorial group was fittingly severe in its lines and appropriately sombre in mood, creating with its sanctuary-like setting an atmosphere of peace and repose, while responding to the City Hall itself in the curving apsidal form of the screen.

Bottom left: *The Cenotaph, photographed in November 1929 [Hogg Collection, Ulster Museum]*

Below: *The War Memorial viewed from the front [Author, 2006]*

Bottom right: *The War Memorial viewed from the rear [Author, 2006]*

Subsequent to Thomas's rearrangement of the grounds in the 1920s, there have been added three more monuments of art-historical interest. The first was the American Forces Monument, a short column of Portland stone designed by T. F. O. Rippingham of Belfast, deputy chief architect of the Northern Ireland Department of Works and Public Buildings. It was carved by Purdy and Millard, and unveiled by the Duke of Abercorn, Governor of Northern Ireland, on 26th January 1943.[125] A modest and understated monument, it was erected to commemorate the landing of the USA Expeditionary Force in Belfast and their first arrival in the European theatre of war exactly one year earlier in 1942. It bears the badges of the United States Army, Marine Corps, and Navy.

Originally it was set up at the boundary in front of the Queen Victoria Memorial, but later moved back when main entrance gates were erected in the 1990s.

The second addition was the Titanic Memorial erected to commemorate those Belfast lives lost on the great passenger liner in 1912. Commissioned from Sir Thomas Brock in 1912, its completion was delayed due to the First World War. A very evocative and melancholy piece, it depicts a female figure, who may be identified as Fame, holding a laurel wreath in her right hand and looking down at two sea-nymphs rising from the waves and supporting in their arms the body of a drowned seaman, all carved in white Carrara marble. The oceanic theme of the

Right: American Forces Monument of 1943 [Author, 2006]

Far right: The Titanic Memorial of 1920 by Sir Thomas Brock, in its original location in the roadway in Donegall Square North [Hogg Collection, Ulster Museum]

Far left: *The Titanic Memorial in its present position in the east garden of the City Hall [Author, 2006]*

Left: *The Pirrie Memorial by Bertram Pergram shown here in its original location in Belfast City Cemetery; it was moved to the City Hall grounds in 2006 [Author, 1986]*

carved work was continued in a really fine pair of bronze drinking fountains to the front and back of the pedestal in the form of dolphins' heads, ornamentally treated, which unfortunately were removed some years ago and were not replicated accurately by their replacements. The monument was one of the last works of Brock, who was too frail to be able to travel to the unveiling by the Lord Lieutenant of Ireland on the 26th June 1920. In fact he died two years later.[126] Originally set up in the roadway in Donegall Square North, the monument was brought into the grounds to a position on the east side of the City Hall in 1960.

The third and most recent addition, over-looking the Titanic Memorial from a position close to the north end of the east façade of the City hall, is the Pirrie Memorial. It commemorates Lord William Pirrie, Chairman of Harland & Wolff and the man largely responsible for the creation of the Titanic, Lord Mayor at the time of the City Hall competition, and one of the committee which specified the original requirements for the

building. All in bronze, it consists of a portrait bust by the London sculptor Bertram Pergram, set on a pedestal which is decorated with plaques depicting the Royal Victoria Hospital which Pirrie was also instrumental in building, and the SS. Venetian, the first ship to be built by the Harland & Wolff company. Illness, incidentally, had prevented Pirrie from joining the Titanic on her ill-fated maiden voyage. Originally set up over Pirrie's grave in Belfast City Cemetery on Falls Road after his death in 1924, this memorial was brought here in 2006.

The last significant change to the City Hall grounds, apart from the wholesale remodelling of Thomas's Garden of Remembrance and the laying out of new pavements, was their complete enclosure by gates and railings, something which Thomas himself had always considered to be "the first important step in connection with the re-forming of the grounds" but which had been deferred in the 1920s.[127]

THE ARCHITECT

At the time of winning the competition for the City Hall, Alfred Brumwell Thomas was a virtually unknown young architect practising under the name of his father's firm. By the time the building was completed he was not only known as one of the most successful and flamboyant practitioners of the revived English Baroque style but he was also soon to be elevated to the higher ranks of society, being knighted in the King's birthday honours in 1906, at the early age of 38, in recognition of his services in connection with the City Hall.[128]

His beginnings had been comparatively humble. Born in 1868, the son of Edward Thomas, a district surveyor working in Rotherhithe, he had studied at the Westminster School of Art and at the Architectural Association in London and travelled in such countries as France, Italy and Holland, before commencing practice in 1894 in partnership with his father.[129] Following his father's death he worked independently, adding the invented name Brumwell as a distinguishing feature, and was joined in the office by his younger brother Ernest Montague Thomas, who had been articled to him in 1896 before becoming his assistant from 1902 to 1910.[130]

Prior to the Belfast City Hall competition Brumwell Thomas had enjoyed moderate success as an architect with such buildings as Huddersfield Sanatorium (1894-7) and the West of England Eye Infirmary at Exeter (1895-7), the latter a lively free Classical design in red brick and terracotta, while his work on the Addey and Stanhope Science Schools in London (1896-8), designed in a dignified red brick Classical style, dates from the same time as his work in Belfast. However, these were all buildings of limited scope, but with his competition success at Belfast he displayed his ability to design on a really grand scale, eventually producing one of the most important public buildings of its period anywhere in the British Isles. His reputation was made, and during the long course of construction at Belfast he was successful in competitions for two other large buildings of similar type, Plumstead (later designated Woolwich) Town Hall (1899-1906) in south-east London, and Stockport Town Hall (1904-8) in Cheshire. Both were designed in a similar idiom to Belfast and faced in the same material, Portland stone, but were nowhere near as expensive, being less grandiose, Woolwich costing £85,000 while Stockport cost £70,000. He

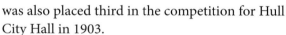

was also placed third in the competition for Hull City Hall in 1903.

Woolwich is a rich essay in the English Baroque style, Ionic columned, with a dominant clock tower to one side and a comparatively subdued dome to the front. It contains a long entrance hall of amazing grandeur, presenting a series of three domes in a row, with a marble statue of Queen Victoria by Pomeroy standing at the head of the grand staircase, while the domed Council Chamber is reminiscent of Christopher Wren's architectural style. The commission for Woolwich fell entirely within the period of Belfast City Hall, construction starting in February 1903 and the building formally opened on 13th January 1906.

Stockport is an equally confident essay in the Baroque style with a majestic main front. Like Woolwich, the exterior is Ionic columned and dominated by a clock tower, which, in its final form, is reminiscent of parts of both the drum and the turrets at Belfast. Inside, the principal staircase is lined with marble panelling similar to Belfast, below a series of saucer domes, while the Council Chamber is also roofed by a dome to very grand effect.

Thomas's last significant building in the Baroque style, and the one which drew to a close the glory days of the Edwardian era, was the public library in Deptford, London, of 1911-14, for at the age of forty-six he interrupted his career as an architect, to volunteer in the First World War and serve from 1914 to 1916, during which time he achieved the rank of major.

Returning to practice after the war, he was responsible for designing such buildings as the Skefco ball-bearing works at Luton (1919), a war memorial at Dunkirk (1923), extensive additions to the Elizabeth Garrett Anderson Hospital in London (1919), and Clacton Town Hall in Essex (1931). This last town hall was designed in a conventional and restrained neo-Georgian style in brick with stone dressings, and lacked the bravura of his Edwardian work.[131] The great age of unrestrained architectural grandeur in civic monuments was clearly over, but there was one last stylistic flourish left in the interesting and unusual design of 1932 by Thomas for the Nizamiah Mosque in London, domed and minaretted in a traditional eastern Islamic style; however it was never built.

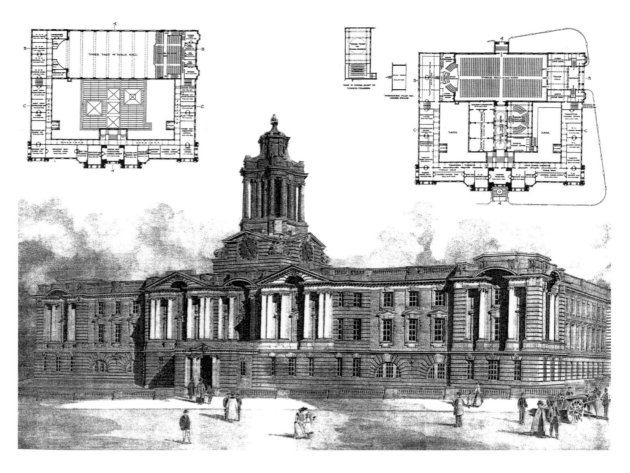

Right: *Stockport Town Hall: Thomas's competition winning design [from* Building News, *1904]*

Then, following an unsuccessful entry in the competition for Hammersmith Town Hall in London, he retired in 1938.

In his professional life Thomas was a member of the Council of the Royal British Colonial Society of Architects, a fellow of the Royal Institute of British Architects, and sometime President of the Architectural Association, while his special connection with Belfast led to his being the RIBA representative on the Ancient Monuments Advisory Committee for Northern Ireland.

Of well-groomed and handsome appearance, judging from his portrait photograph of 1906, he appears to have been of likeable character, remembered with obvious affection by his obituarists.[132] In particular, he had many friends in Northern Ireland and visited Belfast fairly frequently up to the time of his retirement from practice, it being his invariable custom to call on

Far right: *Thomas's design for the Nizamiah Mosque in London [from* The Builder, *1932]*

his old friend James Gamble, Chief Architect in the City Surveyor's Department, at the City Hall where the two had been professional colleagues for almost nine years. His last visit was in July 1947 when he made a tour of the public buildings in the city.

Indeed Thomas's architectural interest in Belfast extended beyond the commissions he received in connection with the City Hall and its grounds. In the early 1920s he offered his views on improving the city and made a number of suggestions for re-shaping its appearance.[133] He recommended that the new Parliament House should have been sited in the city centre, in the markets area, with a terrace on the River Lagan, flanked by the Royal Courts of Justice on one side and Government administrative buildings on the other, rather than being situated at Stormont on the outskirts, a view which he pressed on Northern Ireland's first Prime Minister, Lord Craigavon but without success. It was Thomas's belief that the outward and visible sign of government was most important in a new State and that Belfast had been generally unfortunate in the past in the placing of its public buildings and squares.

He also proposed that a great public space be created near St Anne's Cathedral; that a luxury hotel be built in Donegall Square East,[134] a project for which he provided drawings at his own expense; and that traffic islands and roundabouts be created in the main streets, with statues placed in them, removed from the City Hall grounds, suggesting for example that the Dufferin Memorial be moved to the centre of Shaftesbury Square.

Sir Alfred Brumwell Thomas died on 22nd January 1948, at Holloway Sanatorium, Virginia Water, Surrey, in his eightieth year. He never married and had lived with his sister for much of his life, while his architect brother had died many years before, in 1917. Brumwell Thomas was an important figure in the architectural establishment in Britain in an age when traditional values reigned supreme and no expense was spared in extravagant and imperial monuments to civic pomp and pride, but one who owed his spectacular rise to fame and his ultimate professional success to his involvement with Belfast City Hall.

Above: *Perspective drawing of 1907 of Belfast City Hall as completed [from Building News, 1908]*

EPILOGUE

Previous Page: View through the circular light-well of the main entrance hall towards the great dome [Author 2009]

Already described as a 'great building' even before it was finished,[135] the City Hall was acclaimed at the time of opening in 1906 as 'a magnificent edifice, worthy in every sense of the rank which Belfast holds amongst the cities of the Empire, and a fitting centre for its municipal enterprise'.[136] Its cost, as first proposed, had been almost doubled, not without considerable public outcry and opposition in the process, but when it was finished, and 'visible in all its grace and majesty' as one critic put it, any adverse criticism 'died into silence and left only contentment and admiration'.[137] In any case, it was well known that the interest and the sinking fund expenses had been paid out of the profits of the local gas industry and not out of the rates. As was proudly noted at the time, this palatial building could be fairly regarded as 'symbolising the wealth and importance of the community'.[138]

Aside from its purely practical and functional value the new building had provided the city with an architectural centrepiece of the highest merit, and created for it a new heart. As one critic observed, 'it centres and dominates the city –

giving this the character and atmosphere it has been so long wanting'.[139]

Clearly a success from a local perspective – 'a complete and satisfactory realisation of all their hopes and ambitions' as one admirer said at the opening in August 1906[140] – its achievement was also acknowledged elsewhere, Brumwell Thomas being knighted later on that year for his personal part in the building. It was all the more unfortunate then that this glorious climax should have been followed by a somewhat sour note the next year when Thomas served a writ on the Corporation for £13,000 odd, the balance of his fees, according to his personal and rather unrealistic interpretation of the contract, beyond the £8050 he had already received, and was offered a sum of only £7,000 in settlement, which the Corporation believed was not only fair but generous.[141]

Relations were strained once again on Thomas's return to the city some years later when his engagement by the Corporation to prepare designs for the rearrangement of the City Hall grounds, including the layout for the Garden

Below: Panoramic view of the City Hall and grounds from the north-east in 1906 [MBR, Belfast]

Left: 'The City Hall
Under Snow', painted by
William Conor, c1920s
[Collection of the Ulster
Museum, by courtesy of
The Conor Estate]

of Remembrance, was considered by them to be on an informal basis only. When Thomas complained of a lack of a proper contract he was dismissed in 1927 for breach of agreement but his designs were retained. He was then blamed for delays in constructing the war memorial, unfairly it seems, and he felt compelled to defend his reputation in a letter to the press.[142]

Notwithstanding these unhappy episodes, involving disagreements over fees and conditions of contract, the association of Thomas with Belfast and the project for a new city hall was a fortunate one for its architectural impact. Built in the heyday of the city's rise to commercial power in an era of supreme self-confidence, this iconic and inspirational building became the chief architectural glory of Belfast, a status it still retains today. Standing at the heart of the city and seeming to draw all Belfast towards it, this epitome of Victorian endeavour and apogee of Edwardian sumptuousness brought architectural drama to the city centre.

Above: *The City Hall as viewed from the north along Donegall Place c1908 [MBR, Belfast]*

Opposite: *Aerial view of Donegall Square from the south-west showing the City Hall and the Garden of Remembrance [by courtesy of F.W. Boal]*

Of monumental sculptural quality outside and with a masterly manipulation of spaces within, this is a magnificent building, the most important of its era in Ireland, one of the grandest examples of the Baroque Revival anywhere in the British Isles[143], and arguably the greatest town hall of its time. A perfect expression of the prosperity and civic pride of the city at the turn of the twentieth century, Belfast City Hall is the complete embodiment of Edwardian splendour and still dominates the city over a century after its opening.

ENDNOTES

INTRODUCTION

1. Hitherto the fullest account of the architecture of the City Hall has been the illustrated monograph published at the time of opening – Sir D. Dixon, Sir S. Black, and A.B. Thomas, *The City Hall of the County Borough of Belfast. A monograph in three chapters*, Belfast, 1906. Other contemporary accounts were A.B. Thomas, 'The Belfast City Hall', in *Architectural Review*, Vol 20, October 1906, pp187-208; and 'The New City Hall, Belfast', in *Irish Builder and Engineer*, 11 August 1906, pp657-662 (with supplementary reports, including corrections, and illustrations, in 25 August 1906, p678; 8 September 1906, pp718, 728, and illustration f. p712; 22 September 1906; p753 and illustration f. p764); and *The Builder*, 18 August 1906, pp233-5. For architectural descriptions since then see the following: A. Trimble, *Guide to Belfast*, Belfast, 1911, pp14-24; R.M. Sayers, *Belfast Telegraph guide to Belfast and surrounding districts*, Belfast, 1934, pp9-19; C.E.B. Brett, *Buildings of Belfast*, London, 1967, pp54-56; and P. Larmour, *Belfast: an illustrated architectural guide*, Belfast, 1987, pp60-61.

2. The materials for an architectural history of the City Hall are found in the record of the Corporation's Improvement Committee minutes, held in the Public Record Office of Northern Ireland; in contemporary newspaper and architectural press reports over the period of building; and in a number of surviving original architectural drawings held by the City Council and in PRONI. A useful summary of the building of the City Hall is 'Belfast's City Hall, The scheme and the site. Historical review', in *Belfast Evening Telegraph*, 31 July 1906, p65 [but unpaginated], taken from the *Council Year Book*, for 1906-7, written by Robert Meyer, chief clerk to Belfast Corporation.

3. As reported in *The Builder*, 17 April 1852, p245.

4. As reported in *Dublin Builder*, 15 November 1866, p270, and *Irish Builder*, 15 January 1867, p21.

5. *Irish Builder*, 1873, p56.

6. For the White Linen Hall see B. Walker and H. Dixon, *No mean city: Belfast 1880-1914*, Belfast, 1983, pp24 and 25, and *In Belfast town 1864-1880*, Belfast, 1984, p26. It may be added that in 1849 the premises hosted a linen exhibition which was visited by Queen Victoria and the Prince Consort, and on that occasion Prince Albert, the Prince Consort, formulated the idea which culminated in the Great Exhibition at London in 1851.

7. As reported in 'New City Hall for Belfast. The erection postponed', in *The Ulster Echo*, 5 October 1893.

A GREAT ENTERPRISE

8. Consisting of the Lord Mayor William McCammond, Lord Mayor elect William Pirrie, Alderman R.J. McConnell (chairman), Alderman Thomas Brown (vice-chairman of the Improvement Committee), and Alderman Lavens Ewart.

9. Such as Manchester Town Hall (1868-77) and the Natural History Museum, London (1873-81). For Waterhouse see C. Cunningham and P. Waterhouse, *Alfred Waterhouse 1830-1905*, Oxford, 1992.

10. As for example in *The Irish Builder*, 15 July 1896, and *Building News*, 10 July 1896.

11. There is a copy of Bretland's sketch plans in PRONI (catalogue no LA7/8JA/2/1-4).

12. For editorial comment and architects' correspondence on the matter see *The Builder*, 8 August 1896, p114; 15 August 1896, p134; 22 August 1896, pp152 and 156 (letter from William Young); 29 August 1896, p175 (letter from Charles Barry); 5 September 1896, p193 (letter from R.F. Chisholm); 12 September 1896, p216 (letter from J.M. Brydon); 26 September 1896, p254 (letter from John Belcher); and *The Irish Builder*, 15 August 1896, p173.

13. *The Irish Builder*, 1 October 1896, 203.

14. As reported in *The Builder*, 7 November 1896, p385. It may be added that the designs submitted were placed for the inspection of the Council in "the large room" at the gas works. (*Belfast Telegraph*, 31 July 1906, p6). A complete list of competitors is not available but the names of the following are known – E. Thomas and Son of London; Stark and Rowntree of Glasgow; James Miller of Glasgow; Graeme-Watt and Tulloch of Belfast; W. Fennell of Belfast; F.W. Lockwood of Belfast; Clark and Hutchinson of London; S. Henry Eachus of Wolverhampton, and Humphrey and Hopkins. It is uncertain if Henry Hare of London entered or not: a drawing by him published by the *Architectural Review* in 1896-7 as a design for Belfast City Hall was actually a design for a school or college.

15. The irregular proceedings were reported in *The Builder*, 21 November 1896, p429, and 5 December 1896, p464, and *Building News*, 4 December 1896, pp805-6, and were commented upon by Thomas Drew in his presidential address to the Royal Institute of Architects of Ireland which was reported in *The Irish Builder*, 1 January 1897, p1. Any reference to this controversial and unedifying episode was omitted from subsequent summaries of the City Hall competition.

16. Graeme-Watt and Tulloch (sometimes identified as Watt and Tulloch) were a well-known Belfast firm, the senior partner Robert Watt (who later adopted the surname Graeme-Watt) having been responsible for designing on his own a number of jobs for the City Corporation in the late 1880s to early 1890s, such as the Public Baths at Falls Road (now demolished), at Ormeau Avenue, and at Templemore Avenue, and the Gas Works Offices on Ormeau Road. With Tulloch he was architect for the East Bridge Street power station (now demolished) which was formally opened the same day as the City Hall foundation stone was laid.

17. For example in *The Builder*, 5 December 1896, p470, and *The Irish Builder*, 1 December 1896, p243.

18. As reported in *The Builder*, 12 December 1896, pp491-2, and *Building News*, 18 December 1896, p897.

19. As reported in *The Builder*, 19 December 1896, p519.

20. See *Building News*, 11 December 1896, p865; 18 December 1896, p898; 1 January 1897, p45, and 8 January 1897, p78.

21. *The Builder*, 3 April 1897, p320.

22. As reported in *The Ulster Echo*, 1 April 1897.

23. *Ibid*.

24. *The Builder*, 12 June 1897, p534 and illustrated supplement, and *Building News*, 18 June 1897, illustrated supplement.

25. *The Irish Builder*, 10 October 1901, supplement f, p896.

26. For Stark and Rowntree's see *Building News*, Vol LXXII, 25 June 1897, and *Academy Architecture*, 1899, p106; for James Miller's see *Academy Architecture* 1898, p82; and for Graeme-Watt and Tulloch's see *Building News*, 23 July 1897, p113 and illustrated supplement.

27. See H.H. Statham, *Modern Architecture*, London, 1897, p107 (illustration reproduced from *The Builder*).

28. See H.H. Statham, *op cit*, p68 (illustration reproduced from *The Builder*).

29. See *Building News*, 10 November 1882, and *The Builder*, 11 November 1882.

30. *The Builder*, 12 June 1897, p534, and *Irish Builder*, 10 October 1906, p896.

31. Namely the east front by Le Vau, Perrault, and Le Brun, 1667-70.

32. For example in a book such as A.H. Macmurdo, *Wren's City churches*, 1883, and in a lecture such as 'The English Renaissance', by J.M. Brydon, given at the Architectural Association in London in February 1889 (and published in *The Builder*, 23 February 1889, pp147-8, and 2 March 1889, pp168-170).

33. See *Building News*, Vol XLVII, 1884, p300.

34. See *The Builder*, 2 May 1885 and *The British Architect*, 27 November 1885, p230 and illustrated supplement.

35. See *The Builder*, 18 June, 1887, for Brydon's design, and H.H. Statham, *Modern architecture*, London, 1897, p122 (illustration reproduced from *The Builder*), for Leeming and Leeming's design.

A DREAM PALACE

36. As quoted in 'Forty years after' by Sir Brumwell Thomas, in *Belfast News-Letter*, 1 August 1946, p3.

37. As reported in *Irish Builder and Engineer*, 18 August 1928, p7, when £5,000 had been voted towards the cost, and 29 August 1931, pp749-750, when it had been estimated it would cost £35,000 to complete the work.

38. As chief architect to Belfast Corporation, James Gamble was later to design such buildings as the former Gas Show Rooms, corner of Gresham Street and North Street (1908), Ligoniel Public Baths (now Public Library), Ligoniel Road (1910), and Belfast East Power Station, Wolff Road (1919-23, but now demolished). He was responsible for later additions to the City Hall, such as the pedestal for the bust of J. C. White designed for the principal first floor landing in 1923, and the extensive basement accommodation along the south wing designed in 1932. He died in 1956.

39. Reported in *The Northern Whig*, 3 November 1898, p6.

40. *Ibid.*

41. *Ibid.*

42. The City Hall was one of the first examples of a great public building to which the Plenum and Paul Vacuum systems combined, was applied. The Plenum system and the Paul Vacuum system of forced air were combined for the Great Hall, the Banqueting Hall, the Reception Room, and the Council Chamber, while the low pressure radiator system was used for all corridors, halls, vestibules, staircases, and larger offices. A great deal of attention had been devoted to the question of heating and ventilating, and a deputation from the Council had visited buildings in England, Scotland, and Dublin to inspect the most recent developments. Among other modern services and equipment installed in the building were two passenger lifts, one in the south-east corner and the other in the north-west angle close to the Council Chamber; synchronised clocks; and a system of telephones for internal communication between offices and direct lines to outside, run from an exchange located immediately to the west of the entrance vestibule.

43. The event was written up in the *Belfast Evening Telegraph*, 18 October 1898, p5; *Belfast News-Letter*, 19 October 1898, p6; and *Northern Whig*, 19 October 1898, p5. The *Belfast News-Letter's* account was reprinted along with a rare photograph of the proceedings in James Henderson, *A Record Year in My Existence as Lord Mayor of Belfast, 1898*, Belfast, 1899.

44. The full contents were listed in *Belfast News-Letter*, Wednesday 19 October 1898. The voices on the phonograph were recorded in Committee Room B of the old Town Hall, on the previous Monday, by a representative of the Edison-Bell Consolidated Phonographic Company.

45. *Belfast News-Letter*, 19 October 1898, p6.

46. Thomas was credited with their design in 'The new City Hall. Laying the foundation stone', *Belfast News-Letter*, 19 October 1898.

47. As reported in *The Northern Whig*, 3 November 1898, p6.

48. *Ibid.*

49. *Ibid.*

50. Illustrated and described in *The Irish Builder*, 1 January 1900, p227 and supplement f p226. Sculptural detail indicated within the porch was to be changed yet again in final execution.

51. From 'Minutes of Improvement Committee', 25 August 1903. Thomas had intended originally that the four corner cupolae would also be covered with lead but that was later changed to copper.

52. *The Irish Builder*, 1 July 1900, p41.

53. *The Irish Builder*, 10 October 1901, p896.

54. Although *The Irish Builder*, 10 October 1901, p896 reported the tender as £25,600.

55. Sir Brumwell Thomas, 'Forty years after', *Belfast News-Letter*, 1 August 1946, p3.

56. From 'Minutes of Improvement Committee', March 1903.

57. *The Irish Builder and Engineer*, 14 January 1905, p6.

58. See 'From a lady's point of view', in *Belfast News-Letter*, 2 August 1906, p8.

59. The event was written up in the *Belfast Evening Telegraph*, 1 August 1906, p3; *Belfast News-Letter*, 2 August 1906, pp7-8; *The Northern Whig*, 2 August 1906, p8.

60. *Belfast News-Letter*, 2 August 1906, p8.

61. *The Northern Whig*, 2 August 1906, p8.

62. The words of the ode were recorded in full in the *Belfast Evening Telegraph*, 1 August 1906. It was written by a Mr W. Livingstone, and set to music by Dr Koeller, conductor of the Belfast Philharmonic Society, and not written by Samuel Cowan as has been stated in G. McIntosh, *Belfast City Hall: one hundred years*, Belfast, 2006, p40. What Cowan wrote was 'Verses on the unveiling of the [Queen Victoria] statue' in 1903.

63. *Belfast News-Letter*, 2 August 1906, p9. The woodcarving was all by Purdy & Millard of

Belfast, while the stained-glass was executed by two firms from Belfast: Ward & Partners, and Campbell Brothers. Ward & Partners were responsible for all the principal windows, namely those in the main staircases and the public rooms, and the lunette of the principal first floor landing. Their contract was the largest public order for stained-glass paid for by public money ever given to an Irish firm and was particularly arduous as only a little over two months was allowed for it. Campbell Brothers meanwhile were responsible for the windows in the peristyle of the dome; decorative leaded lights in internal doors and fanlights; leaded glazing in the angle towers, the porticoes buttressing the great dome, and the attic of the dome; and leaded lights in the ground floor hall, and principal first floor landing, some of which were subsequently removed to make room for later memorial windows.

64. The occupancy of the building for practical municipal business had not yet begun. Departments were scheduled to be transferred from their previous premises on the 1st of September.

65. See *The Irish Builder and Engineer*, 8 September 1906, f. p712, and 22 September 1906, f. p764; and *Architectural Review*, Vol 20, October 1906, pp187-208.

EXTERIOR OF THE BUILDING

66. It was supplied by the Bath Stone Firms Ltd from the John Pearce Quarries on the island of Portland in Dorset.

67. Chambers (1726-96) was the greatest official architect of his day in England, exerting great influence in British architecture as head of the profession and through his numerous illustrated publications such as his *Treatise on civil architecture* (1759). Somerset House (1776-86) was his largest and best known work.

68. Vincenzo Scamozzi (1552-1616), an Italian architect, was the most important of Palladio's followers. His publication *L'idea del' architettura universale* (1615), the last of the theoretical works of the Renaissance, exercised a wide and lasting influence in Northern Europe.

69. Gibbs (1682-1754), a Scottish born architect who trained in Rome, was the most influential London church architect of the early 18th century. He exerted great influence in British architecture generally, partly through his profusely illustrated *Book of architecture* (1728).

70. John Vardy (d 1765) was an English architect of the Palladian school who was Clerk of Works at Greenwich subsequent to Wren's involvement there. Spencer House (1756-65) is his most important surviving work: illustrated in R. Blomfield, *A short history of Renaissance architecture in England*, London, 1900, f p188.

71. For Pomeroy (1856-1924) see F. Pearson, 'Pomeroy, Frederick William', *The dictionary of art*, ed J. Turner, London, 1996; and M. Stocker, 'Pomeroy, Frederick William', *The Oxford dictionary of national biography*, Oxford, 2004. Pomeroy was engaged for the City Hall pediment in December 1901 at a fee of £2000.

72. Winter (1875-1937), was a stone and wood carver in Belfast who was involved in other buildings in the city centre such as Ocean Buildings (1899-1902) in Donegall Square East, the Presbyterian Assembly Hall (1902-05) in Fisherwick Place, and 36-38 Donegall Place (1903).

73. *The Irish Builder and Engineer*, 11 August 1906, p661. It had been previously criticised, in a very facetious manner, in *The Irish Builder and Engineer*, 7 October 1905, p694.

74. The carved work on the capitals of the angle towers was executed by H.H. Martyn & Co of Cheltenham.

75. Cherubs' heads appear on Wren's St Paul's, outside and inside, and on some of his churches, such as the frieze of St Mary-le-Bow tower doorway, as well as over the windows of Gibbs's church of St Mary-le-Strand.

76. Gibbs's porch at St Mary-le-Strand (1714-17) was itself probably based on the semi-circular porches by Wren on the transept fronts of St Paul's, which in turn may have derived from the façade of da Cortona's church of S.Maria della Pace in Rome (1656-9).

77. The basement accommodation along this south side appears to have been inserted to the designs of James Gamble of the City Surveyor's office in 1932, its windows based on those of Thomas's original small basement below the east staircase which faces into the courtyard.

78. *Belfast News-Letter*, 2 August 1906, p10.

79. The Bromsgrove Guild was credited in the list of contractors given in contemporary sources at the time of opening (see note 1 above) such as the 'Monograph' by Thomas et al, the *Belfast News-Letter*, and *The Irish Builder and Engineer*, with "modelling". Their main activity in other jobs at the time was highly modelled ornamental plasterwork as at Thomas's Woolwich Town Hall, and it would appear that they were responsible for the same here, but another speciality of the Bromsgrove Guild at the time was ornamental rainwater goods. In the absence of any other contractor listed in this field at Belfast, we may suppose that the Bromsgrove Guild were also responsible for the moulded lead hoppers; they may well also have been responsible for the modelling of cherubs for the bronze electroliers which were cast by the bronze founders J. W. Singer & Sons.

INTERIOR OF THE BUILDING

80. Traditionally the main marbles in the City Hall have been given as Pavonazzo and Brescia following a description of the building while in progress, which was written by A.B. Thomas and published in *The Irish Builder and Engineer*, 14 January 1905, p6. His reference to Brescia, a place name in Lombardy, was incorrect and misleading, however, the proper term for the marble in question being 'breccia'. Breccia is a mottled marble, composed of various sized angular fragments of marbles or hard stones cemented together by a matrix of another colour which forms veins. Both Breccia and Pavonazzo (a yellowish white marble heavily veined with shades of gold, purple, blue, and black) are found in the Apuan Alps, otherwise known as the Carrara Mountains. Thomas's erroneous term has continued through all later descriptions of the City Hall down to the present day. See also note 84.

81. For MacDowell (1790-1870) see H. Potterton, *Irish church monuments 1570-1880*, UAHS, Belfast, 1975, p58, and T. Snoddy 'Patrick MacDowell' in J. Hewitt, *Art in Ulster: 1*, Belfast, 1977, p170.

82. Rome and Co's work here at Belfast was under the direction of a Mr A. Law; the decorative elements were presumably cast from clay models provided by the Bromsgrove Guild of Worcester.

83. *The Northern Whig*, 2 August 1906, p8.

84. Carrara is a name loosely used to designate marbles coming from the area around the town of that name in Tuscany. It is popularly intended to mean, as Thomas did in his own descriptions of the City Hall, the white or white-veined-grey type from that area.

85. The 'historic treatment' of the stained-glass windows was conceived by the Belfast architect and historian, Robert Magill Young, at the invitation of the City Council in 1905.

86. *The Northern Whig*, 2 August 1906, p8.

87. The principal first floor landing is sometimes erroneously referred to as the 'Rotunda', presumably because of the circular lightwell and the dome above, but the term should only be applied to a room which is itself circular in plan; this room is rectangular. The term was not used here by Thomas himself.

88. Thomas's precise source or direct inspiration for this idea of an open circular well in a floor underneath a large dome is not known and appears not to have been speculated on before, but a precedent can be found in the Second Church of the Invalides in Paris, known as 'The Dome Church', built in 1692-1704 to the designs of J.H. Mansart, which had a circular crypt created in it by direction of a later architect Visconti to receive Napoleon's tomb, completed in 1861, which could be viewed from above through the well. Another instance is to be found in the Kunsthistorisches Museum in Vienna of 1872-91, by Gottfried Semper and Karl von Hasenauer, where the domed hall has a balustraded circular floor well opening to view the entrance hall below.

89. Cipollino means onion-like markings. Ignored by the Greeks, this marble was prized by the Romans who quarried it on Mount Carystus in Euboea and used it widely in Rome and in their North African colonies such as Carthage, where many of the columns were subsequently reused in modern Tunisia in churches by Byzantine architects, and later reused again in Islamic monuments such as the great Mosque at Khairouan.

90. Brindley had an academic interest in marbles as well as a commercial one, presenting such papers on the subject as 'Marble: its uses as suggested by the Past', *Transactions of the Royal Institute of British Architects*, Vol III, New Series, 1887, pp45-56, with accompanying plates. In this paper Brindley indicated, at p48, that "good Cipollino is now again obtainable". The marble work at the City Hall was supervised on behalf of Farmer and Brindley by Thomas Monks. Prior to being brought over to Belfast these columns were put on display in London where they were "pronounced by competent judges to be amongst the best specimens ever seen of this particular kind of marble", as reported in *Belfast News-Letter*, 2 August 1906, p9.

91. As embellished with vases the form of these open-pedimented archways may be compared with Wren's timber screens to the west end of St Paul's, with the materials and the order changed.

92. For Luke see T. Snoddy, 'John Luke', in J. Hewitt, *Art in Ulster: 1*, Belfast, 1977, p166; and J. Hewitt, *John Luke (1906-1975)*, Belfast, 1978.

93. See the *Belfast Evening Telegraph*, 12 July 1906, p6. The statue was transferred from the Public Library around June 1906, at the request of the Earl of Shaftesbury, and placed against the angled face of the south-east corner in the main entrance hall of the City Hall.

94. Presumably the bust exhibited by Pomeroy at the Royal Academy in 1921.

95. Presumably the bust exhibited by Merrifield at the Royal Academy in 1941.

96. *Belfast News-Letter*, 28 June 1920.

97. The name 'Whispering Gallery' was used here first by Brumwell Thomas in his description of the building in progress published in *Irish Builder and Engineer*, 14 January 1905, p6.

98. Cartoons for some of these signs and symbols were illustrated in *The Belfast News-Letter*, 2 August 1906, p10 and others in the *Irish Builder*, 23 January 1907, p129.

99. Drawings for the restoration of the great hall were prepared in 1949 by Smyth and Dorman, architects of Belfast.

100. Their involvement is recorded in J. Whitaker, *The best: a history of H.H. Martyn & Co*, Cheltenham, 1998, p74.

101. The design for the central window depicting Queen Victoria was provided by John Bewsey of London who exhibited it, along with designs for the peristyle of the dome and the lunette above the principal staircase, at the Royal Academy in London in 1906; presumably it was he who was also responsible for the other portrait windows, at least, in the Great Hall. Another English artist Hugh Arnold exhibited a design for stained-glass for the City Hall at the Royal Academy in 1905, but the subject or location of the window was not specified.

102. Illustrated in *Some Historic Donegal Carpets*, 1912, and in P. Larmour 'Donegal Carpets', *Irish Arts Review Yearbook*, 1990-1991, pp210-216. Previously, at the time of opening of the building, Donegal carpets, made by Alexander Morton and Company, had been used for the staircases and various public rooms.

103. *Belfast Telegraph*, 1 July 1924, p10; *Belfast News-Letter*, 2 July 1924 and *Northern Whig*, 2 July1924, p7.

104. Other original furniture designed by Thomas, apart from tables and chairs for committee rooms and the fixtures in the Council Chamber, included stationery chests, clerks' desks and large roll-top desks for departmental offices.

THE GROUNDS

105. McKimm was credited with preparing the gardens in the *Belfast News-Letter*, 2 August 1906, p10, and 1 January 1908, p11.

106. For Brock (1847-1922) see M. Stockler, 'Brock, Sir Thomas', *The dictionary of art*, ed J. Turner, London, 1996, and 'Brock, Sir Thomas', *The Oxford dictionary of national biography*, Oxford, 2004.

107. See the *Belfast News-Letter*, 28 July 1903 for a report on the ceremony and an historical record of the project. It may be added that the quadrangle of ground in front of the main entrance in which the memorial is sited was dubbed 'The Queen's Lawn' by Charles McKimm, the park's curator (*Belfast Evening Telegraph*, 1 August 1906).

108. Sir Brumwell Thomas, 'Forty years after', *Belfast News-Letter*, 1 August 1946, p3.

109. *The Irish Builder and Engineer*, 30 July 1903, p1884, and 13 August 1903, p1916.

110. *The Irish Builder and Engineer*, 11 August 1906, p661, and 25 August 1906, p684.

111. *Belfast News-Letter*, 15 May 1924.

112. *Belfast News-Letter*, 7 October 1905, and *Building News*, 13 October 1905, p529. The original site for the monument had been granted in October 1903.

113. See 'The Dufferin Memorial', *Belfast News-Letter*, 9 June 1906, p8 for a history of the project and a perspective sketch for the monument, almost exactly as executed. Additionally it may be noted that the bronze figure of 'Canada' was exhibited by Pomeroy at the Royal Academy in 1904, and a model of the overall monument was exhibited there in 1906 (illustrated in *Academy Architecture*, 1906, p25).

114. *Belfast News-Letter*, 2 August 1906, p9.

115. *Belfast News-Letter*, 1 January 1908, p11.

116. R.M. Young in W.T. Pike ed, *Belfast and the Province of Ulster in the 20th century*, Brighton, 1909, p110.

117. *The Irish Builder and Engineer*, 11 August 1906, p661.

118. *The Irish Builder and Engineer*, 25 August 1906, p684.

119. A. Brumwell Thomas, 'The Belfast City Hall', *Architectural Review*, Vol. 20, 1906, pp187-208.

120. See photograph in *Belfast Telegraph*, 16 May 1924, p12.

121. See the *Belfast News-Letter*, *Belfast Telegraph*, and *The Northern Whig*, 15 May 1924.

122. The detailed design for the completion of the war memorial and the arrangement of the steps following Thomas's dismissal was by Young and Mackenzie, architects of Belfast. Their design was illustrated in the *Belfast News-Letter*, 21 February 1929. Their engagement followed an abandoned competition advertised in November 1928 for a terminal finish to the cenotaph.

123. Although the original intention in the 1920s according to a leaflet 'Brief description of the War Memorial and the Garden of Remembrance' published on completion would appear to have been to cultivate plantings – "The full effect of the Memorial cannot yet be realised, but with care in the gardening layout and in the preparation of the soil to allow of the better growth of trees, plants, and flowers, the Garden of Remembrance will quickly assume a very beautiful aspect". The cruciform arrangement of paths appears in drawings by James Gamble of the City Surveyor's Office as early as 1929.

124. *The Irish Builder and Engineer*, 18 April 1925, p314 (tenders of W.J. Campbell and Son received); and 20 August 1927, p606 (photographs of completed work).

125. See the *Belfast Telegraph*, 25 January 1943 (photograph showing stone carver at work on the monument), and 26 January 1943 (report on unveiling).

126. See the *Belfast News-Letter*, 28 June 1920, p6. Additionally it may be noted that Brock exhibited 'The 'Titanic' memorial for Belfast – group' at the Royal Academy in 1916.

127. 'Belfast City Hall … Letter from Sir B. Thomas', *Belfast News-Letter*, 23 February 1927. Ornamentally treated gates and railings were eventually set up in the late 1990s; at the same time a bronze and stone memorial was set up to the west of the Queen Victoria Memorial to commemorate the awarding of the Victoria Cross to Leading Seaman James Magennis.

THE ARCHITECT

128. As reported in 'Knighthood for the architect of the City Hall, Belfast', *The Irish Builder and Engineer*, 17 November 1906, p927.

129. For Alfred Brumwell Thomas see A.S. Gray, *Edwardian architecture: A biographical dictionary*, London, 1985, pp347-8; A Service, 'Thomas, Sir Alfred Brumwell', *The dictionary of art*, ed J. Turner, London, 1996, Vol 30, pp742-3; and P. Larmour, 'Thomas, Sir Alfred Brumwell', *The Oxford dictionary of national biography*, Oxford, 2004.

130. E.M. Thomas (1878-1916), who was present at the official opening of the City Hall in 1906, left his brother's office in 1910 to become assistant to the consulting architect to the Government of India, where he died. See obituary in *The Builder*, 12 January 1917, p36.

131. For a description and illustrations of Clacton Town Hall see *The Builder*, 17 April 1931, pp707, 717-719.

132. J.G. Gamble, *RIBA Journal*, April 1948, pp271-2; *The Irish Builder and Engineer*, 7 February 1948, p98; 'Obituary: Sir Brumwell Thomas', *Belfast News-Letter*, 26 January 1948.

133. 'What might have been? Plan for a brighter Belfast', *Belfast News-Letter*, 23 June 1955.

134. *The Irish Builder and Engineer*, 4 October 1924, p869.

EPILOGUE

135. *The Irish Builder and Engineer*, 14 January 1905, p6.

136. *Belfast News-Letter*, 2 August 1906, p7.

137. *The Irish Builder and Engineer*, 11 August 1906, p657.

138. *Belfast News-Letter*, 2 August 1906, p9.

139. *The Irish Builder and Engineer*, 11 August 1906, p661.

140. The Earl of Shaftesbury, as reported in *Belfast News-Letter*, 2 August 1906, p8.

141. See *The Irish Builder and Engineer*, 20 April 1907, p286; and the *Irish News*, 4 June 1907, p5, and 13 June 1907, p5. Aside from various expenses, Thomas was claiming not only 5 per cent on the entire expenditure on the completed building, but also 3 per cent on the amount of the first contract which he contended had been abandoned. In the event he accepted the amount which Belfast Corporation had lodged in court in Dublin. The builders H. & J. Martin, incidentally, were reported to have sought a sum of £67,000 but settled in the end for £33,000.

142. See 'The Garden of Remembrance. Sir Brumwell Thomas's engagement terminated', *The Irish Builder and Engineer*, 1927, p92; and 'Belfast City Hall … Letter from Sir B. Thomas', *Belfast News-Letter*, 23 February 1927.

143. Other important examples besides those referred to previously include the following, all domed – Old Bailey Criminal Courts, London (1900-06) by Edward Mountford; Cardiff City Hall (1897-1906) by Lanchester, Stewart and Rickards; the Ashton Memorial, Lancaster (1904-09) by John Belcher; the Mersey Docks Building, Liverpool (1903-07) by Arnold Thornely; and, beyond the British Isles, but by a British architect, the Queen Victoria Memorial, Calcutta, India (1903-21) by William Emerson.

APPENDIX

List of those involved in the building and furnishing
of the City Hall in its original phase, 1896-1906.

Architect – Alfred Brumwell Thomas, London

Clerk of Works – James G. Gamble, Belfast

Sculptor – Frederick Pomeroy, ARA, London

General Contractors – H & J. Martin Ltd, Belfast

Sub-contractors:

Carving – Purdy and Millard, Belfast; H.H. Martyn & Co. Ltd,
Cheltenham; J. E. Winter, Belfast.

Marble Work – Farmer & Brindley, London

Mosaic Pavings – Diespeker, Ltd, London.

Wood Block Flooring – Ellis, Geary & Co, London

Plasterwork – George Rome & Co, Glasgow

Modelling – The Bromsgrove Guild, Worcester

Stained-glass – Ward & Partners, Belfast; Campbell Brothers,
Belfast

Constructional Steelwork for Dome – Clyde Structural Iron Co,
Glasgow

Constructional Steelwork for Flooring – P & W MacLellan,
Glasgow

Heating and Ventilation – Ashwell & Nesbitt, Ltd, London

Hot Water Service – Musgrave & Co, Belfast

Electrical Work and Hydrants – William Coates & Sons, Belfast

Lifts – William Coates & Sons; The Medway Lift Co, London

Plumbing and Sanitary Work – John Dowling, Belfast

Electric Fittings – J. W. Singer & Sons, Frome

Wrought Ironwork – Francis Ritchie & Sons, Belfast

Clocks – Gibson & Co, Belfast

Strongroom Doors – Milner & Sons, London

Safes – Thomas Skidmore & Sons, Wolverhampton

Carpets and Blinds – Gillespie & Woodside, Belfast

Furniture – H & J. Martin Ltd, Belfast; Goodall, Lambe &
Heighway Ltd, Manchester; Maguire & Edwards, Belfast;
Hampton & Sons, London; Partridge & Cooper, London.

Glossary of Architectural Terms

Amorino: winged baby or young child, also called a cherub or putto; amorini in plural

Apron: raised panel, sometimes shaped and ornamented, below the sill of a window or niche

Architrave: lowest division of an entablature; also the moulded frame around a door or window

Arcade: a range of arches supported on piers or columns

Balustrade: railing protecting the edges of stairs, balconies, terraces or roofs; composed of balusters or short posts with handrail or capping

Baroque Architecture: architecture of the 17th and part of the 18th centuries that is characterised by exuberant decoration, curvaceous forms and a preference for spatially complex compositions

Baroque Classicism: term which denotes baroque architecture where restrained modelling of wall surfaces was preferred to more extravagant swelling and curvilinear forms

Baroque Revival: phase of architecture in late 19th to early 20th centuries in which the forms or ornamentation and spatial characteristics of the original baroque style were re-created

Blocking course: plain course of stone surmounting a cornice at top of a wall or colonnade

Breakfront: slight projection in centre of a façade rising the full height of the building

Buttress: projection from a wall to strengthen it or counter any outward thrust.

Carolean: relating to the period of King Charles II in late 17th century

Cartouche: panel or tablet with ornate frame, usually with incurved scrolling

Classicism: revival of, or return to, the principles and stylistic features of Greek and Roman architecture, often inspired at second hand by the classical trends of the Renaissance

Colonnade: row of columns carrying entablature

Colonnette: small column

Corinthian: classical order in which capital has two rows of acanthus leaves below row of modest volutes

Cornice: projecting section of a classical entablature

Cupola: small dome crowning a roof or turret

Diocletian window: semi-circular window divided into three lights by two vertical mullions

Doric: classical order characterised by a simple and austere column and capital

Drum: cylindrical sub-structure of a dome

Entablature: upper part of an order, consisting of an architrave, frieze and cornice

Exedra: in classical architecture, a vaulted termination, usually semi-circular, to the end of a room; extrae in plural

Fluting: vertical grooves or channels cut into the shaft of a column

Frieze: the middle division of an entablature, between the architrave and cornice; also, a horizontal band of ornament running around a room immediately below the ceiling.

Ionic: classical order in which the capital has two large volutes scrolls to the top

Lugged surround: architrave whose top is prolonged at each side into ears or lugs; also known as shouldered.

Lunette: arched or circular opening for a window

Loggia: covered outdoor space, open on one or more sides and usually forming part of a building

Mannerist: relating to a 16th century style of architecture in which classical elements were used in a strange or abnormal way

Neo-classical: a strand of classical revivalism that derived inspiration directly from antique Greek or Roman sources rather than indirectly from the Renaissance

Neo-Palladianism: 18th century revival of Palladian architecture

Oeil-de-boeuf: small round or oval window; also called an oculus or bulls-eye-window

Ogee: double curved form of convex and concave parts

Order: the system, in classical architecture, of columns, capitals and bases and the entablature which they support.

Palladian: in the style of the 16th century Italian Renaissance architect Andrea Palladio

Palladian Window: tripartite window consisting of a central semi-circular arched light flanked each side by narrow rectangular openings; also called Venetian window.

Pediment: low pitched gable of triangular or curved form to the top, above a portico or door or window

Peristyle: a range of columns surrounding a building

Piano-nobile: main floor of a building, containing the reception rooms, usually on an elevated level

Pilaster: shallow flattened version of a classical column and capital projecting only slightly from a wall

Pile: large upright post usually of timber or concrete driven into soft ground to support a superstructure

Porte-cochère: porch large enough for wheeled vehicles to pass through

Pulvinated: convex in profile; cushioned

Renaissance: rebirth or revival of ancient Roman standards and motifs in art and architecture, which started in Italy in the 15th century and spread to other European countries

Rusticated: boldly cut in blocks separated from each other by deep joints; a rusticated column has a shaft interrupted by projecting blocks

Shouldered: see lugged

Spandrel: the area of walling between two arches or between an arch and its containing rectangle

Stylobate: the steps or substructure on which a portico or colonnade stands

Tuscan: the simplest of the five Roman orders, with a plain base and capital and unornamented frieze

Venetian Window: see Palladian window

Wainscot: the timber lining to internal walls

Index

ILLUSTRATION CREDITS

Illustrations marked 'PRONI' are reproduced by courtesy of the Public Record Office of Northern Ireland and Belfast City Council.

Photographs in the collections of the Ulster Museum are reproduced by courtesy of the Trustees of National Museums Northern Ireland. The painting of 'The City Hall under snow' by the Belfast artist William Conor in the collection of the Ulster Museum is reproduced by kind permission of The Conor Estate.

Photographs credited to 'NLI' are reproduced by courtesy of the National Library of Ireland.

Photographs credited to 'MBR' are from the Monuments and Buildings Record of the Northern Ireland Environment Agency.

Photographs credited to Baird's 'Monograph of the City Hall', 1906 are taken from the following publication – Sir Daniel Dixon, Sir Samuel Black, and A. Brumwell Thomas, *The City Hall of the County Borough of Belfast. A Monograph in three chapters,* W&G Baird Ltd, Belfast, 1906.

Photographs credited to 'Author' are by Paul Larmour.

WHAT IS AI?

NEAL LAYTON

Hodder
Children's
Books

Do you know what the most **COMPLEX** thing in the known universe is?

I'll give you a clue – you've got one!

It's not a smart phone,

or instructions for building a super mega space rocket,

or even the tangle of socks in your drawer . . .

It's your BRAIN!

Right now, you are using your ears if this book is being read to you, or your eyes if you are reading it yourself.

But it is your brain that is sorting the signals sent from your ears and eyes, moving your attention around the page. (While probably having **THOUGHTS** like, 'What *is* he going on about?')

Human brains are AMAZING!

It's because of our **AMAZING** brains that over the many years since humans first appeared, we have spread across most of our planet.

Big brains have also helped us humans to **INVENT** lots of things to make our lives easier. Clothes, houses, farmed food, transportation, chocolate bars and many different types of machines – including computers.

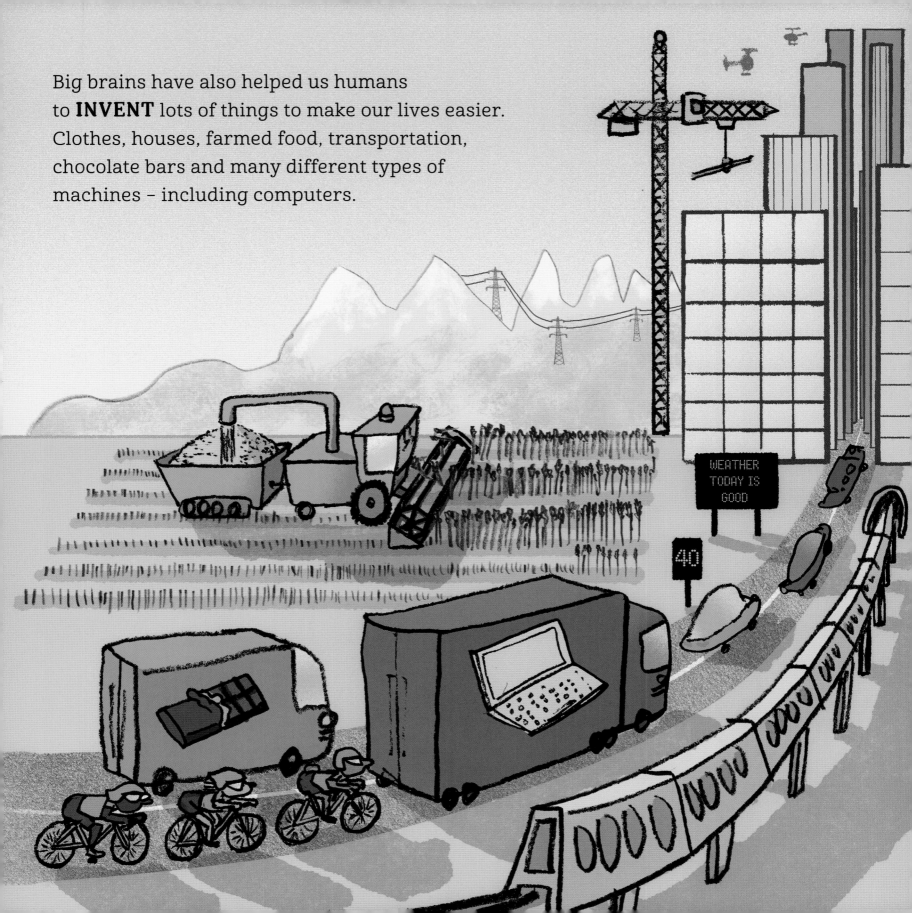

A computer is a **MACHINE** that can be instructed, or programmed, to do specific tasks.

The first computers could only do one thing, like solve difficult number sums.

Charles Babbage, clever inventor an mathematician

Ada Lovelace, brilliant mathematician

Hardware is the bits of a computer you can touch.

But then came the bright idea of making a computer that could use lots of different programs. These early computers were usually **VERY** big.

Software is the programs* on computers that allow them to do multiple things.

* a list of instructions in special computer language that tells the computer what to do.

The idea caught on, and over the years, computers got faster and faster and smaller and smaller.

Now there are **MINICOMPUTERS** in just about everything.

PLAYER 1   PLAYER 2

Modern multi-use home computers can do hundreds of different things, often at the same time. The different programs in multi-use computers are often called applications, or **APPS**.

20°

1:15

SUPER wash

As computers got better, the programs
that ran on computers also got better.

Then one day, people wondered, 'What if we didn't have to give the computer instructions to follow? What if we made a computer that could come up with its *own* ideas, and learn by itself, just like a **HUMAN BRAIN?**'

This is called AI, which stands for:

ARTIFICIAL (built by humans)

INTELLIGENCE (the ability to have ideas and learn)

You might not realise it, but there are tiny bits of special AI computing *already* in . . .

Smartphones

Online music players

Search engines

Smart televisions

Online shops

So, how do they work?

Well, a bit like the way your brain learns, AI programs love to gobble up information. This information is called **DATA,** and AI programs take in lots and lots of it.

Then the AI looks for **PATTERNS** in the data. Repeating patterns can be found everywhere: in shapes, colours, numbers, words and even sounds!

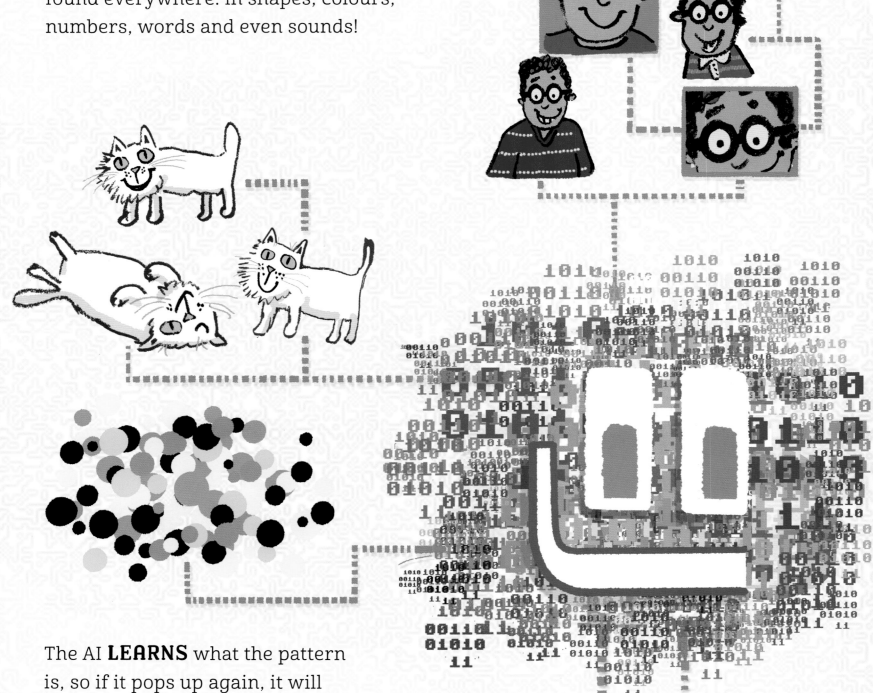

The AI **LEARNS** what the pattern is, so if it pops up again, it will recognise it.

The AI then puts the information it has collected back together in different ways, creating shiny **NEW** ideas.

The AI we have today is very clever,
helping us do many complicated tasks . . .

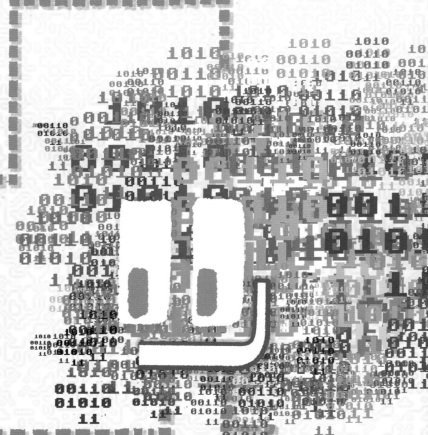

but it still finds some things difficult!

And so far, nobody has made anything as
complicated as a whole **HUMAN BRAIN,**
which can do lots of different types of thinking . . .

lots of different types of learning . . .

and learn from its thinking and learning, leading in turn to more learning.

So, what would happen if somebody did actually, eventually, make a computer brain that was as good as a human one?

HOW CAN I HELP YOU TODAY...?

It could be really useful and help humans to do all sorts of things.

But computers, even the ones we have at the moment, can do things really **FAST**. So, if a computer brain could think and learn, it would be able to think and learn really fast too. Faster than you or me.

And if it could learn really fast, it might become clever very quickly. It might become **cleverer** than the people that made it, even **clevererererer** than the **BRAINIEST** people on Planet Earth. This could be *really* useful.

But if an AI superbrain could *really* think for itself and outsmart the smartest person on Earth . . .

could it end up telling humans what to do, rather than the other way around?

In fact, the idea of making a computer brain that can really **THINK** and **LEARN** raises lots of questions, like:

If humans made a superbrain that knew **EVERYTHING,** would we still need to go to school?

If humans made a superbrain that was clever enough to write and illustrate books like this one, would we need writers and illustrators anymore?

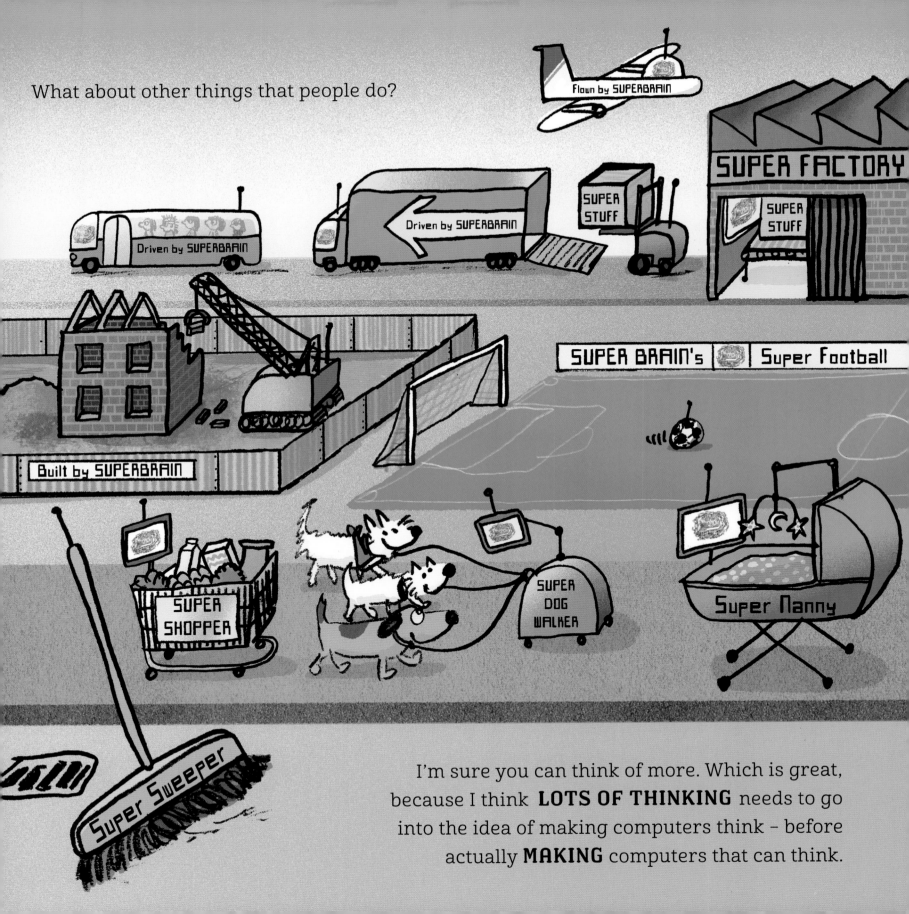

What about other things that people do?

I'm sure you can think of more. Which is great, because I think **LOTS OF THINKING** needs to go into the idea of making computers think – before actually **MAKING** computers that can think.

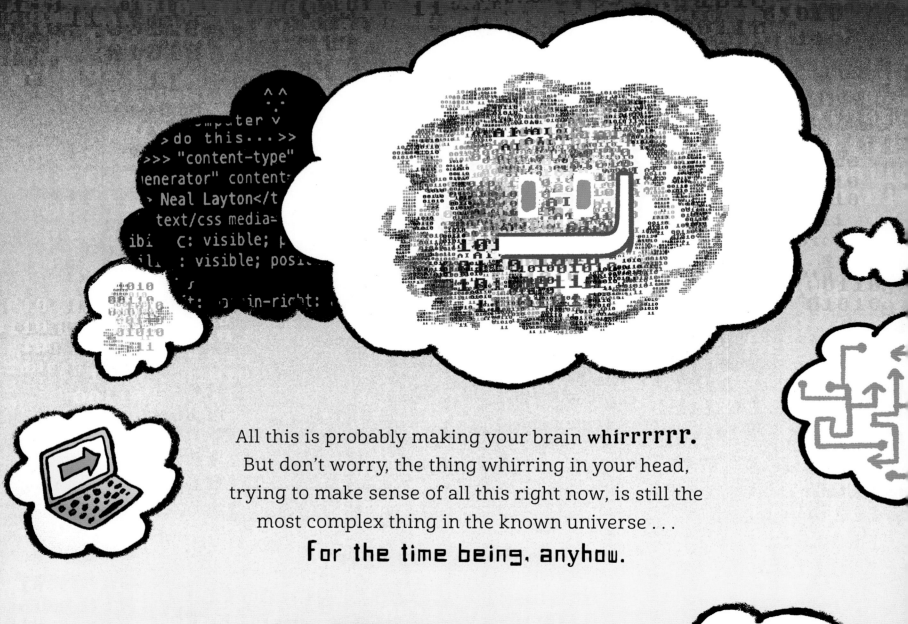

All this is probably making your brain **whirrrrrr.**
But don't worry, the thing whirring in your head,
trying to make sense of all this right now, is still the
most complex thing in the known universe . . .
For the time being, anyhow.

For Mum, Dad and my ZX81 ~ N.L.

HODDER CHILDREN'S BOOKS
First published in Great Britain in 2024 by
Hodder and Stoughton

Copyright © Neal Layton, 2024
With thanks to AI consultant Jonny Brooks-Bartlett

PB ISBN 978-1-444-97558-1
E-book ISBN 978-1-444-97559-8

1 3 5 7 9 10 8 6 4 2

Printed in China

MIX
Paper from
responsible sources
FSC® C104740

Hodder Children's Books
An imprint of Hachette Children's Group
Part of Hodder and Stoughton Limited
Carmelite House, 50 Victoria Embankment, London, EC4Y 0DZ

An Hachette UK Company
www.hachette.co.uk
www.hachettechildrens.co.uk